Mary F. Wright

1972

Randall Elementary

School

The Elementary School

L
E
A
R
N
I
N
G

C
E
N
T
E
R

for Independent Study

The Elementary School

LEARNING CENTER FOR INDEPENDENT STUDY

Joyce
Fern
Glasser

Parker Publishing Co., Inc.
West Nyack, New York

© 1971, by

PARKER PUBLISHING COMPANY, INC.
West Nyack, New York

Library of Congress
Catalog Card Number: 73-148512

Printed in the United States of America
ISBN 0-13-259713-6
B & P

DEDICATION

In memorium and tribute to my father:

Daniel D. Glasser

Because of the positive impact of his life upon many,

and most especially upon me and my life's work.

The Value of This Book. . . .

Innovation—a new idea—should never be a finalized product. It should be an exciting, worthwhile challenge continually demanding man's creative energies to build it and make it grow. To me, the Learning Center concept is just that kind of challenge. This book, therefore, is not the only way to establish a Learning Center. Rather, it conveys the how of beginning and what has resulted from the employment of Learning Center dynamics.

Having used traditional teaching and testing techniques, it has been exciting to change to the Learning Center approach and watch the harvest of youngsters eager to learn and behaving responsibly about it. In other words, aggressive learners rather than passive students is the way it ought to be—and it can be done. Thus, this book will be of practical value to the educator who desires to initiate and/or develop a Learning Center. It will help you regardless of the construction of an individual school building—no matter what its library facility, no matter what its financial circumstances. Before going further, however, I would like to stress the fact that the Learning Center is not so much a place as it is an idea. It is more than an elementary or secondary school library or resource center. It is more than a place housing books, materials, multimedia, chairs, sofas, desks, etc. Most

7

importantly, the Learning Center represents an idea—an idea that works, an idea that adds a significant dimension to a youngster's education by heightening the individual's desire to learn.

The Learning Center concept is keyed to helping youngsters develop certain behaviors within an atmosphere of freedom—an absolutely necessary milieu. These behaviors are: to evidence increased ability in decision making regarding one's own learning program; to be able to make increasingly more appropriate selections of materials with which to help oneself to learn; to exhibit tenacity; to be able to fail without a sense of hopelessness; to demonstrate the desire for ever-increasing responsibility for one's own learning progress; to be able to work independently; to demonstrate ways of applying what one has learned; to find joy in learning and to find the paths that lead to successful, self-rewarding achievement. Ways have been discovered to organize the Learning Center to accomplish these goals, without the chaos that freedom often brings.

Unique features of the Learning Center program are: it is an *organized* program for the individualization of instruction, and, as a place, it is where friends may choose to work as learning partners (an option indicative of independent study); it is a place where a youngster assumes the responsibility for his learning progress; it is a place where youngsters may be found working on the floor in a group, or singly on a sofa or at a desk.

A review of the origin and development of the Learning Center will be found in the Appendix, and for those who have worked closely in the development of the Learning Center concept, it becomes increasingly evident that one day the Learning Center may, in fact, become a total school concept. This book deals in larger measure with an understanding of this concept, the factors that led to its development, Learning Center practices today and practical methods for implementation.

Joyce Fern Glasser

Acknowledgments

Sylvia Glasser, my mother, for her encouragement.

Joyce Morris, Guidance Counselor in Barrington, Illinois, for her human insights and counsel.

Helen Jameison, Learning Center Director at the Juliet Lowe School, District 59, Illinois, for supplying valuable materials contributive to the scope of this book and for the work she added regarding IPI.

Jack Arbanas, Learning Center Director at North School, Glencoe, Illinois, for his unstinting help.

Walter Johnson, formerly a Model Program Coordinator for Learning Centers with District 59, Elk Grove Village, Illinois, for assistance with the Appendix and for other valuable materials resulting from his work as Model Program Coordinator in Elk Grove.

Richard J. Bodine, Director of the Service and Demonstration Center for Program Development for Gifted Children, Lakeview High School, Decatur, Illinois, for his fine contribution on independent study included in Chapters 7 and 8.

Diane Schwartz, Learning Center Director, Darien, Connecticut, for her very helpful contributions.

Dr. Paul Lawrence, Superintendent, Elgin Public School System, Elgin, Illinois, for giving me the opportunity for leadership to innovate.

J.F.G.

Contents

Contents

1

Developing a Sound Basis
for the Learning Center

DEVELOPMENT OF LEARNING
CENTERS IN ELK GROVE

The schools in Elk Grove School District 59 were first introduced to the Learning Center concept in 1963. The superintendent at that time, Dr. Roger Bardwell, was a man of vision and foresight who sought innovation for the school district. He was often quoted when he said, "Change is good, any kind of change." He felt that through change people were exhibiting enough flexibility to perhaps improve the schools for children.

One of the innovations was the concept of the Independent Study Centers at the new Salt Creek School. Miss Charlotte Levens was appointed principal of the school, a school that would be built to provide centers for independent study. Later that year, a few other schools implemented centers in their buildings. Each year a few more centers were adopted in existing school buildings, as well as being built as a part of the new buildings.

Today, all but one school has put a Learning Center into operation. Their viability depends upon the degree of staff involvement in making them increasingly meaningful and integral to the productivity of the schools. Money, then would continue to be no object.

GOALS AND OBJECTIVES OF THE ELK GROVE LEARNING CENTERS

The purpose of the Learning Centers in the Elk Grove District 59 Schools is to provide and encourage an instructional program in independent study.

For a long time educators have ignored what psychologists have said about the learning process. Most often, schools have been built and new programs introduced for administrative convenience rather than for student or learner needs. The new principles of learning are too often put second to administrative convenience, as is the case in homogeneous grouping.

We already know that intrinsic rewards are more conducive to learning than extrinsic rewards, a view contrary at least initially to those of the behavior modification school. When we look at children in various situations—schoolrooms, gym, music, scouts, parks, backyards, etc.—we have often observed that they are far more likely to become enthusiastic in projects they, themselves, have participated in planning and selecting. Excessive direction by the teacher or other adults is likely to result in apathetic conformity, defiance, scapegoating or escape from the situation (drop-outs). Changes in organizational patterns, curriculum materials and new technology will not induce change in learning techniques, especially if teachers try to keep their traditional patterns of behavior and expect students also to maintain their passive roles as learners.

It can be assumed that students are more likely to grow in their ability to assume responsibility for their own learning if they are given something to say about what they learn and when they realize the logical outcome of the fun of discovery and self-reliance. In Elk Grove's Learning Centers, students have learning options available to them that will help facilitate a program in independent study. An independent study program, therefore, provides freedom, security and built-in success factors. It allows students an opportunity to make choices or options. If you have an independent study program, you must provide the students with options associated with learning experiences. They must be able to decide their scheduling (how much time), with whom they wish to study, where they wish to study and what they wish to study. And a teacher, in the guidance role, can assist children in these decisions. Also, these choices or options must be something that both the students and the teacher are aware of as options.

For the most part, schools have attempted to provide for the development of student responsibility through organizational innovations. Usually these innovations do little more than permit the student who is capable of making decisions to have a limited degree of opportunity to become responsible for his own learning decisions.

Most of the independent study programs and learning centers have been at the junior high level and beyond. Elementary programs are steadily and rapidly increasing through philosophical commitment and money-saving techniques such as differentiated staffing.

In the several years of Learning Center history in District 59, one of the most significant steps forward was the development of a philosophical statement and the concomitant purposes, goals and behavioral objectives for Learning Centers. (It cannot be contended, however, that the form of the statement is unassailable.)

During the months of September and October 1967, the Learning Center teachers met to compose this organizational statement. It was framed in view of District 59's key goal. . .to individualize instruction. While the statement is by no means to be construed as absolute, nonetheless, it is functional and a prerequisite must. It serves in organizing a school's program, in training a school's staff, in identifying Learning Center direction to parents, etc.

LEARNING CENTER GOALS

The Learning Center aims to provide a school framework within which the individual child may procure the guidance, climate and media to learn and find purpose and joy in learning. Opportunities are provided for the individual's learning needs and for creating and developing his interests.

The child must be guided in using these opportunities to choose materials and join activities that will provide a learning challenge and success. In addition, it is our aim to help the youngster to evaluate his goals. The pupil is encouraged to broaden and deepen his learning horizons, and to become increasingly responsible for his learning decisions.

PURPOSES–GOALS–OBJECTIVES

I.   *To Provide the Climate for Self-Actualization.*

A.   **Experience joy in learning.**

1.   Unsolicited verbal expression of pleasure.
2.   Perseverance in projects.
3.   Demonstrates physical signs of pleasure.
4.   Pursues interests.
5.   Eager to share experiences.
6.   Displays ability to concentrate, maximum involvement.
7.   Readiness to pursue task.
8.   Shows pride in wanting to display work, achievements, satisfactions.

B.   **Develop or broaden academic and/or aesthetic interests.**

1.   Self-initiation of research through the use of card catalog, reference books, seeking outside sources, field trips, audio-visual, vertical file and other materials (process).

Student makes collection, presentation, bulletin board, builds or manipulates a model, foreign language, puts on a play, writes own programs, teaches others, makes own audio-visual materials (product).

2.   Chooses to become involved in aesthetic interests through listening to records or tapes, looking at artwork, attending per-

formances of music, art, dance, poetry (process).

Student creates own music, poetry, plays, stories, artwork, crafts (product).

C. **Develop self-reliance and independence.**

1. Diagnose and prescribe for his own learning needs.

   a. identifies an area(s) for improvement.

   b. can locate, **operate and** will choose to use appropriate materials.

2. Function as an individual in a group setting.

   a. exercises self-discipline.

      1. identifies tasks, engages in production behavior.

      2. is sensitive to needs of other members of group.

D. **Develop self-awareness.**

1. Provide atmosphere for free questioning (accepting and nonthreatening atmosphere).

   a. accept child's judgment.

   b. be positive.

   c. allow child to make choices.

E. **Encourage self-acceptance.**

1. Providing encouragement to a child to continue to work to his capability and accepting his limitations.

2. Learning to accept and apply his academic and aesthetic talents.

II. *To Provide an Instructional Program Geared Toward Independent Study Through Student Options.*

A. **Content options to choose media based on:**

1. Depth of interest.

2. Level of ability.

3. Individual needs.

B. Grouping options.

    1. Child may choose to work with group.
    2. Child may choose to work alone.
    3. Child may choose to work with teacher.

C. Pacing

    1. Child may work at his own speed.
    2. Child may work with no predetermined deadline.

D. Evaluation.

Option of:

    1. Self-evaluation.
    2. Conferring with director for evaluation.
    3. Conferring with classroom teacher.
    4. Conferring with peer group for evaluation.

III. *To Act as a Resource and Service Center for the School and Community.*

A. Screens and evaluates for the purpose of recommending media.
B. Keeps up to date with new materials.
C. Familiarizes teachers with audio-visual aids.
D. Provides resource materials.
E. Diffuses Learning Center philosophy through training and community presentations.

The foregoing statement of philosophy, purposes, goals and objectives made by the Learning Center teachers of District 59 is particularly meaningful when considered a keystone in the building of a district's unified, yet individualized, approach to conducting Learning Centers. Likewise, a school staff should, at the outset, establish their goals, also. Diverse concepts as to what a Learning Center is and/or should be can wreak havoc upon its successful initiation and operation. When each of, say 16 staff members has his own idea about why a Learning Center should exist, just imagine what could happen if the Learning Center operated with a 17th idea in mind. Such problems have occurred. Communication, unification of purpose, shared decision making are necessary ingredients to productive operation.

Centers have operated without a statement of philosophy, etc. The price to be paid can be called waste. . .of time, money and most importantly, of effective education. An example of economy through goal direction can be studied in regard to this goal statement: *to guide a youngster in finding joy in learning.* To keep waste to a minimum would mean keeping this goal in mind when ordering materials. If, from experience, it is known that youngsters enjoy using certain materials, similar items will be purchased or popular items will be reordered when worn. In other words, time and money will be saved by this approach of using goals as guides to purchasing.

Another example: This same goal would indicate that the Learning Center should reflect a relaxed, though not careless, atmosphere. A center should have carpeting because youngsters enjoy working on the floor. It should have sofas and/or soft chairs because others enjoy learning when curled up. There should be study carrels, for some children enjoy privacy while studying. There should be tables because certain youngsters *enjoy* working in groups of their choosing.

Motivationally speaking, while again using the Learning Center goal of promoting a joy in learning as an example, it is much easier to talk to youngsters when keeping your goals in mind. If a youngster says "I don't feel like using this material anymore," one would make any of these replies: "Why?"; "Is it too difficult?"; "Is it too easy?"; "How long have you been working with it?"; "You mean it's not helping you as you thought it would?"; "Why don't you spend the rest of this period choosing something that will help you improve where you'd like to?"; "The decision is yours on how you'll use your time here—utilize it carefully!"; etc. The approach that these quotes indicate is vastly different than that found in a statement like, "Tom, I think you should continue using the program. Maybe I'll change your program in three weeks, so right now sit down and do what I told you to." In other words, the kinds of learning activities you're encouraging them to do must be those they'll have a choice over (that will encourage their decision-making ability) and which they will consequently *enjoy.*

Another goal that gives a Learning Center program

direction is "to develop or broaden academic and/or aesthetic interest." This goal implies that an Interest Study Program would be an important means of guiding and motivating youngsters toward achieving that goal. In fact, it can be foreseen that a key function of the Learning Center will be in the promotion of an expanded facility in which the youngsters can do, or practice, or build what they've learned about through their interest studies.

This goal and the foregoing description of achieving it implies that books and materials are to be purchased that are: geared to the interests of young children; graphic (even though difficult to read); have an easy accessibility and usability factor and ones the youngsters enjoy using. Equipment to be purchased would include tape recorders, phonographs, individual and group filmstrip viewers; electrical outlet study carrels; manipulative musical devices; easels; etc. Space to be provided would include a quiet working area; activity area; play rehearsal and A-V area; activity labs (science, shop, music, art, home economics, recording studio, etc.). Needless to add, many of these items are assuredly in the deluxe category! (See Chapter 6 for specific recommendation lists.)

Field trips would certainly play a key role in the achievement of such a goal. Visits to concerts, museums, galleries, theatre performances (getting backstage if possible), pottery factories, etc., would help to broaden aesthetic interests.

The three goals C, D and E (to develop self-reliance and independence, self-awareness and self-acceptance) have implications in common. They indicate that the Learning Center should be a place with a relaxed atmosphere. They imply most importantly, however, that the Learning Center teacher and in fact all those associated with the Center be guidance oriented people. It would be assumed that they are oriented this way because of a warm and selfless spirit, one that is understanding of youngsters. This statement should not be construed to mean that such teachers should be lax "disciplinarians." Those educating youngsters must be guidance oriented rather than instructor oriented.

While these examples of goal implications are not comprehensive, nonetheless it must be evident that establishing goals is intrinsic in the establishment of a meaningful, successful Learning Center program. It must be scrupulously kept in mind however, that once established, the goals are not complete. They must be regularly reviewed, developed, enhanced—some dropped perhaps and new ones added. A goal to be added in fact could well be: *to review our goal statements as a staff each year.*

Receiving guidance in every phase of operating through goal direction is, therefore, a practical and effective method of getting things done in such a way as to accomplish what you started out to do. While goal setting may be adequate in and of itself, a philosophical statement has its function too. Through it comes form—a collective statement as to what the Learning Center aims to do. For those who study it and/or compose it, the process becomes the way to a general understanding of what the total operation is to encompass as well as a little better understanding of one's own values. It serves as a mode of explaining to parents and other interested people what is being attempted. It serves as a testing ground for the goal statements (are they what we really want or, conversely, does our philosophy imply all we intend it to?).

THE GOAL CARD

In District 59's philosophical statement it says: "The Learning Center aims to provide a school *framework* within which an individual child may find the guidance, climate and media to learn and find purpose and joy in learning." The Ridge School Learning Center teacher, in September of 1967, developed a tool—one which provided the school with the type of framework that was just mentioned in the quote. This tool was simply a form based on similar ones developed for other situations. The tool's name was the Goal Card. (See Figure 1-1.)

The original Goal Card is different from the one you see here. With the Ridge School staff's help, it has become an

NAME_____

HOMEROOM NUMBER_____

GRANT SCHOOL
GOAL CARD

My goal is to improve in_____.
My goal is to learn a great deal about_____.

Activities that may help me:	MARCH				
	Monday	Tuesday	Wed.	Thursday	Friday
MATH GTT (Graflex Time Telling) GP (Graflex Perimeters) GAF (Graflex Add. of Fractions)	3	4	5	6	NO SCHOOL Teacher's WKSHP. 7
CTB (California Test Bureau) Add.____Sub.____ Mul.____Div.____	10	11	12	13	14
	17	18	19	20	21
READING GRI (Graflex Reading Interpretations) SR (Sullivan Readers) Book____ PL (SRA Pilot Library) Kit IIa____	24	25	26	27	28
Kit IIb____ KS (SRA Kaleidoscope of Skills)	31 Monday	APRIL Tuesday	Wed.	Thursday	Friday
LANGUAGE CTB (California Test Bureau) (English Lang. Sentence Pat.)		1	Spring Recess Begins at 3:00 PM 3	2	NO SCHOOL 4
	Classes Begin Again 14	15	16	17	18
The materials I expect to use are: _____ _____	21	22	23	24	25
_____	28	29	30		

FIGURE 1-1

increasingly more functional, more sophisticated tool. Furthermore, as a tool it does provide structure to a Learning Center Program.

Every other month, the Ridge Learning Center Teacher took a set of new Goal Cards to each classroom. She discussed what a goal is, how one attains it, how the children were coming along, how they could evaluate their progress because of their keeping a record of what they did and where they left off. She talked about the new activities and materials—how they worked and what areas for improvement the materials could service. These group sessions, in other words, served well as a time to continually orient the youngsters to an ever increasing concept of self-integrity—of responsibility for their own learning; as a time to discuss their increasing pleasure in using the Learning Center (that their proper self-placement in programs has brought them success and that as a result they are coming closer to the attainment of the goals to which they had committed themselves in writing upon their Goal Cards); as a time when suggestions are made for Interest Study Projects; as a time when the need for their regular record keeping is discussed; as a time for praising publicly those who have earned commendation; as a time for seeking suggestions for improving the Learning Center; etc. It is preferable of course, if the classroom teacher handles this procedure.

Because of this sort of classroom procedure which requires about 30-40 minutes for each class every two months (more in the beginning), the youngsters require little if any further direction in the Learning Center. They enter the Center and follow these steps:

1. Get their folder or manila envelope (folders are kept in bins for the second-fifth graders and are in alphabetical order).
2. Gather their materials (or on some occasions study the materials in order to make decisions concerning what's best for themselves and those materials which they'd like well enough to stick with for at least a month).
3. Choose their working area (the place suited to their working individually or as a member of a group).

4. Do their work.
5. Mark their Goal Cards on the day they are there, indicating by use of abbreviations the material they've used and where they have left off (Sample: SRA-Bk17-p.76).
6. Put their materials away.
7. Put their folders back.

While the youngsters are working in the Learning Center, the Learning Center teacher, or preferably the classroom teacher, is free to talk with them, give them praise, guide them, encourage them, help them, etc. It is a wonderful role to play and one to which the youngsters readily respond.

PHILOSOPHY FULFILLMENT

One aspect of the Learning Center philosophy has been accomplished. A "school framework"—the Goal Card—has been designed and is functional in the organization of all first-through fifth-grade youngsters. (Ridge is a K-5 building.) They know what they are doing and keep track of their work. Consequently, when they walk through the halls on their way to the Learning Center, the youngsters walk with purpose and direction.

ANOTHER SCHOOL'S LEARNING CENTER GOALS

In Glencoe, Illinois, a determined effort to combine special areas with the library resulted in the construction of a new facility. Thus, a special Learning Center was born at the North School in Glencoe; an interesting and worthwhile Learning Center was built as an addition to an existing school facility. Through broad staff involvement, an enviable facility was designed. It contains a library, multi-media materials, a discussion and/or project workroom, an office, an arts-and-crafts area below (which is large enough to serve as a science lab as well) and a creative dramatics area. These facilities represent a high level of Learning Center concept commitment. And, of course, the proximity of these areas was by no means accidental. In fact, their clustering represents an attempt to provide the greatest number and kinds of opportunities for children to engage in independent activities.

The personnel involved in making this facility work includes a Learning Center Director (Jack Arbanas, a highly talented choice for the position), a half-time librarian, a half-time art teacher, a full-time secretary and volunteer parents serving as clerks, aides and as a talent resource pool. Children from grades kindergarten through sixth use the facilities. They enter as a part of a class at least once a week but more often as an individual or as a member of a small group. Group use is usually scheduled. Individual use is typically on a nonscheduled basis.

The goals of this Learning Center are:

1. To provide opportunities for children to pursue individual interests and projects, either as a result and extension of classroom activities or on the student's initiative.

2. To provide opportunities for children to increase their skills in areas such as reading, mathematics and writing.

3. To provide for new techniques and materials which may be either not economical or ill-suited for classroom use.

4. To provide a variety of enrichment and/or provocative experiences.

5. To provide an opportunity for children to acquire appropriate library and study skills.

6. To provide experiential opportunity of a sort that will enable a student to gain in the ability to use his time "well."

The behavioral objectives are that the student:

* Displays an interest in actively participating in individual or small-group activities.
* Controls his behavior as the situation requires.
* Offers assistance to other children.
* Is increasingly able to schedule his time and activities.

* Is increasingly able to evaluate his own progress.

* Becomes increasingly able to locate and use multi-media materials.

* Uses materials designed to improve specific skills.

* Selects reading books on a variety of themes.

* Reads magazines designed for his age level.

* Listens to poetry and dramatic readings.

* Engages in dramatic activities.

* Becomes cognizant of the works of great composers and artists.

* Uses various arts-and-crafts media to express himself.

* Investigates an expanding range of scientific interests by reading, making collections, conducting experiments.

* Engages on his own in a variety of constructive games and puzzles.

* Is actively interested in displays, special T.V. programs or other enrichment activities.

* Uses the lounge area as a relaxing place to read and wonder.

COMMENTS ON THE NORTH SCHOOL'S LEARNING CENTER

Mr. Frank Maher, principal at North School, has been administratively and ideologically supportive to the creation of this outstanding Learning Center and the goals it represents. This fact is mentioned because his informed support is crucial to the success of North School's Learning Center operation.

Mr. Maher, in cooperation with Mr. Arbanas and other staff members, chose the aforementioned goals in an effort to provide a rather unique Learning Center atmosphere. This atmosphere, which can be described as "relaxed, fun, learning and active," is created by saying to the student, in effect, that any activity selected is as good or as acceptable as any other—a value parity facility. In other words, a student is made to feel

FIGURE 1-2: This Picture Depicts the Stairs That Lead to the North School Learning Center Arts-and-Crafts Facility.

that reading a book is as worthwhile as watching a filmstrip; that watching a filmstrip is as fine as listening to a Beethoven symphony on tape; that listening to a tape is as good as watching the birds eating from the school's feeder; that watching the birds is as much fun as watching the ants scurry along in their ant farm; that watching ants is as worthwhile as playing chess. In fact, this atmosphere also grows from seeing the Center as a haven from the more tight and structured environment, frequently and even at times unavoidably created in the classroom. Certainly classroom demands such as research assignments, remedial work and teacher-selected programs constitute a pressure to engage in specified activities. The Center, on the other hand, intentionally gives the youngster the prerogative of various and exciting choices. Thus, by experiencing real decision making, the youngster has the opportunity to develop a sense of balance between working on those activities he must do (teacher assigned) and those he may prefer to do. Children, like adults, work in spurts and each person best judges his own timing and duration of various activities. In other words, the youngster is being trained to form habits of self-discipline so that he will find himself increasingly more productive.

To provide this full range of choice, worthwhile games such as chess, Mem, Kolah, and three-dimensional tic-tac-toe are an important part of the Center's resources. The games selected are predominantly those that demand skill rather than chance. Some of the advantages of some of these games are that they: provide a quick change of pace; are matches that can be completed in just a few minutes; provide success for many children in an "acceptable" school activity; provide a real problem-solving experience where success is not so dependent on one's reading ability; provide a vehicle for getting to know others in the school in a social setting.

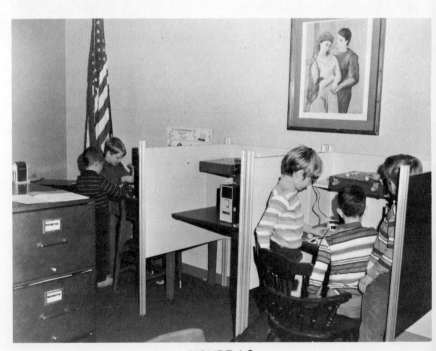

FIGURE 1-3

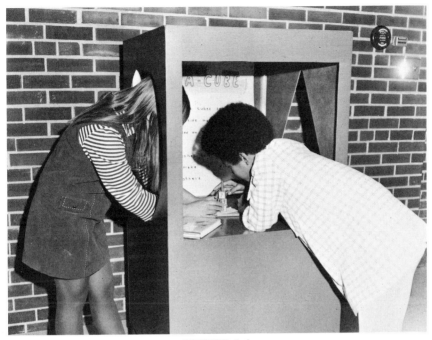

FIGURE 1-4

FIGURE 1-5

From observing North School's Learning Center operation, one has the feeling, and in fact can see, that an important facet of a school's function has indeed been created.

2

Establishing a School's Readiness for Learning Centers

An elementary program of independent study cannot be of any value unless it "works" within a more universal framework. The Ridge School Learning Center's success in suburban Elk Grove was fine. But, what about it working in a more challenging setting? As principal of the Grant Elementary School in Elgin, Illinois, the opportunity was afforded me.

When applying for a principalship in Elgin, a choice was proposed by Dr. Paul Lawrence, the District Superintendent—being the leader of a school in a potentially stable middle-class neighborhood or principal of Grant Elementary School. The administration in Elgin was indeed forthright in clarifying the kinds of problems to be encountered at both schools. Grant was the choice. Grant was the challenge. Grant was described as being racially, religiously and classwise integrated in an approximate proportion to national percentages for each group represented. There were Jews, Catholics, Protestants, Mexicans, Puerto Ricans, Spanish-speaking Americans, Negroes and southern, as

33

well as northern, whites (northern being the larger percentage, which is of course to be expected since Elgin is a northern city). The class structure ran the gamut from very poor lower class to upper middle class.

Equally important in selecting Grant was that for some unknown reason this school had the highest degree of aggressive behavior exhibited by its students than the other Elgin "inner-city" schools. Thus, Grant was indeed the challenge and my choice, on the perhaps naive assumption that if the youngsters at Grant could work well within the framework of Learning Center goals (sound educational goals in the broad sense), then any youngster anywhere could.

Questions at this point could arise; such as: How "rough" is rough behavior? How difficult is a school presenting challenge? From experience in larger schools in the Watts district and in inner-city Chicago, it would have to be admitted that Grant, with an enrollment averaging 305, was not so "rough"—yet, nonetheless, it was challenging!

THE BEGINNING

Upon assessing Grant School's situation in the fall of 1968, the following circumstances prevailed:

1. Before Learning Center concepts could be employed, drastic behavioral changes on the part of students and teachers needed to occur. In other words, the *essential* ingredient for healthy change to occur was nonexistent; i.e., a wholesome, happy *climate.* (Schools where things are really happening have a cooperative, energetic, fun-loving staff and an involved student body.)

2. The youngsters exhibited hostile attitudes and behaviors—name-calling denoting origin was rampant.

3. Minimal teacher supervision duties were required outside of classroom responsibilities.

4. Frequent employment of hostile, repressive, corporal-punishment type techniques were used on chil-

dren to maintain order in the classroom.

5. Some staff members possessed the capability, and were already employing wholesome teaching techniques.

6. Few independent study materials were available, but a hall area designated as a beginning place for a Learning Center was usable.

7. The Grant School image was highly negative—real estate agents recommended other areas to live to parents inquiring about the quality of the school.

8. Most Grant School parents were alienated and hostile toward their school.

9. Practically no expectation prevailed for staff involvement in building (or any form of) goal setting and accomplishment. Typical commentary heard was, "I've got enough to do just running my classroom, without taking on other projects too!"

In other words, Grant School was suffering from a common disease—the cancer spread by teachers who suffer from an inadequate concept of self and whose major goal was to maintain a school setting "like it was" in their day. The hostility thus generated was compounded by students who themselves lacked much positive self-concept definition, and who consequently indulged in the offal of today's common prejudices. (This commentary is a pretty stiff indictment of, among other things, the grim situation fostered by tenure—which, if it exists at all, should be a three- or at most five-year renewable condition.)

While one should feel anger because of the tenure predicament, no hostility should be hurled at any one unfortunate teacher. They too, after all, are the product of an environment. Perhaps, in far-sighted school districts, acceptance will be sought for counseling services unthreateningly offered to teachers. In the meantime, however, we must face the reality of threatened (to the point of relatively little positive action) people—teachers, administrators and parents—and the roadblocks they can't help but place in the way of wholesome change.

SPECIFICALLY SPEAKING

To meet the challenge that Grant School presented (before any Learning Center concepts could be brought about) meant: the employment of wholesome teachers replacing those who left; energetic effort to publicize the "good" things at Grant; dedication to changing our image to one of being a friendly group who made home calls, who showed genuine caring for the youngsters and their parents; involvement of students in helping classmates and school (developing a "proud of the school" type spirit); providing students with operable alternatives to fighting and name-calling; constant effort to establish teacher confidence in administration and a general spirit of openness and trust among all staff members.

Grant School is now a calmer, happier, more productive school where worthwhile, wholesome things can and have been happening for kids. No school can be that way until the basic and frequently unrecognized and unspoken challenge is faced. Dynamic leadership will not be intimidated by it.

STOPPING THE FIGHTING—HOW TO DO IT

To alleviate student fighting, one must recognize that a key cause of the problem is name-calling of the sort that easily reaches a youngster because of his poor,narrow or undeveloped self-concept. When youngsters are merely told that name-calling, or fighting or classroom defiance isn't "nice" and they shouldn't do it or they'll be punished, there is no reasonable foundation for cessation of these negative behaviors. Since in the mind of the child there is no logical basis for limiting or ceasing aggressive behavior, fighting goes on and in fact increases. Then, too, a principal's attitude of, "he'll treat his teacher right or I'll give him a spanking and that'll let him know who's boss around here" exemplifies the sort of authoritarian attitude that may stem fighting, but certainly not hostility nor clever retaliation for such suppression. Whenever discipline assumes the form of "keeping a lid on things," sooner or later there is an explosion with minimal worthwhile learning occurring in the meantime. It can be said without fear of contradiction, therefore, that in the interpersonal relationship of the principal or teacher, the most effective means of approach is through persuasion and certainly not through compulsion. Compulsion promotes primitive attitudes, while persuasion promotes civilizing harmony.

The ingredients necessary to curtail hostility and aggression within a school are basic. In an atmosphere of patience and genuine concern for the welfare of all, one must present rationale to institute the following rules: no fighting; no name-calling; no unsafe activity, either to self or others; keen interest in a school spirit (our school is the best or will be by the time we get through); courtesy that stems from thoughtfulness; rules that have understandable (to the youngster) reasons; a student organization to provide for youngsters helping each other and the school to improve. Easier said than done? Yes, for a while. But time, patience, genuine respect given each youngster as a worthy being and dedication to verbal communication help, and will eventually solve the student-fighting problem. What must happen, therefore, is that the school leader, with the aid of the staff, takes much time with the youngsters to set the standards for the school. He must also take the time to deal with each youngster individually. Nonetheless, if the school leader fails in communicating on a one-to-one basis with the problem youngsters, and finds in addition that perhaps there is no help to be had from the parents, he must not "judiciously" spank the youngster or the program will be hurt at least, or more likely, even be lost. Rather, a dedication to reasoned rather than physical solutions must take place. Sitting with a youngster and trying to establish the real whys and wherefores of an incident is imperative. There is usually no particular need to find out who is at fault, for generally both children concerned are. And, not being witness to the altercation prevents taking sides anyway. So, after each child has had his say, the leader then analyzes what has happened to the youngsters and suggests methods of dealing with the problem should it occur again for the youngsters involved. Methods to be suggested are: staying away from each other; helping them understand that name-calling generally hurts when you think it is the truth; that fighting isn't necessary unless in self-defense where your life is truly threatened. And, finally, that when angry and fighting you have lost because you are doing what your opponent wanted you to do. You are a puppet. You have lost your "cool" and your opponent knows that he has made you look like a fool. This final bit of information is easy for troubled youngsters to understand. Furthermore, it is easy to illustrate. Every youngster has seen angry adults and even angry teachers. How do they look?—Smart? Sharp? On top? The answers here are obvious and so the point is easily made. (An eighth-grade student once told me how much fun her classmates had in figuring out subtle and sometimes not so subtle ways to make their teachers angry because they all had a hearty laugh watching that angry teacher sputter.)

Using these methods of reason, of building self and school community image, helps change a school's atmosphere. Letting parents and children know on a one-to-one basis that you *care*, that prejudice just doesn't seem to be in you is of utmost importance to communicate—and one must communicate these facts by deeds. Finally, it must be remembered that each incident has its individuality and this uniqueness must be found and dealt with. Following is a story which illustrates this.

On the first or second day of school, I saw two little first-grade girls in the hall. Because their physical education class was outside, I asked them what they were doing in the building. One didn't reply but the other did, saying in effect, I don't have to tell you anything if I don't feel like it. My reaction was to ask the rude little first grader to sit in the office. She cried later on but was still fierce and refused to communicate. Her fourth-grade brother saw her in the office and asked her what was wrong. After telling the story—I was elsewhere for the moment—she started crying almost hysterically. I rushed out and her brother glared at me with hate-filled eyes, warning me that I'd better not lay a hand on his little sister or he'd see to it that I got mine. After school, I called the child's mother. She was most distressed about the matter and came to school first thing the next morning.

My secretary told me that the mother had always been cooperative with the school, but was quite unsuccessful in controlling the behavior of her two sons. Plus, I was told that her second-grade daughter had run a protection "racket" while being a first grader. She was protecting her classmates, for a nickel fee each, from her fierce warrior brothers. Until the "racket" was uncovered, she apparently had a very going concern.

Upon conferring with the mother, I could see that she was generating a burden of hate to her children. Nonetheless, I made every effort to convey to her that I *cared* about her youngsters as well as all the students at Grant, admitting, however, that only time would prove me true or phony. The problem with the second grader subsided, because of the mother's support.

In the following months, there were many incidents that brought this woman's fourth-grade boy and me together. (His sister became friendly and was apparently rid of her hostile behavior.) He was quite a fighter, and on one occasion where he kicked a little girl in the stomach for calling him a name, I finally called the mother. I felt that my efforts were not being successful. It was this phone call that "tipped me off" so that I could understand the hate and hostility that this woman's sons so readily conveyed. A conference was held. It was with some trepidation that I anticipated this conference, which was to be composed of a Negro staff member who had some knowledge of the boy's behavior, the mother, the fourth-grade boy and myself. After brief opening comments, the mother asked me to tell her honestly what I thought was causing such continued aggressive behavior on the part of her sons. I started by saying that not being Negro myself it was almost impossible for me to understand just how hard it must be in this country for most Negroes. There was more than a simple amen as a reply to my opening comments. Then, when the opportunity arose, I indicated that the main way to get ahead today is through education—it's a ray of hope for oppressed peoples. And I didn't spare my words in conveying my conviction. The mother interjected occasionally by saying to her boy how right or how important education is. Then, at that point, I reminded the mother of her instructions to me to be honest. She urged me to be so—and I was. I told her that her hate for the prejudiced manner in which many white people treated her was confusing her sons; that her sons came to school to retaliate for the hurt being caused their mother and them. And she saw that this was true. She also realized that she had been glad that her youngsters retaliated so fiercely. I added my feeling that hate destroys us—that prejudice of white for black and black for white was bred in ignorance and was unfair, but that for the sake of her youngsters we couldn't let them go around hating and fighting or they were going to lose out on their education by being in trouble all the time. The message carried.

Since that time this woman's children haven't fought at school, at least not to my knowledge. They seem happy and, though I have given them no test to verify this statement, I'd be willing to bet that they are learning more.

How much time was spent to bring this about? Much! And how many hours were spent on the other problems that youngsters have had? Many! These efforts were well spent however, for Grant School is now much closer to being ready to take the necessary steps in establishing a Learning Center program.

GRANT SCHOOL AS OF NOVEMBER 1969

It could be contended that Grant, under the scrutiny of careful evaluative methods, would now easily rank at about the middle of a chart indicating the degree of a school's aggressive behavior. It is no longer necessary for the Grant Elementary School principal to spend anywhere near the amount of time required in the early months of her administration. Time, in terms of interacting on a one-to-one or small-group basis with youngsters, is now more frequently spent in observing and joining in on study projects and by working with the Council. Some discipline problems for the principal to help with do occur and normally will probably continue to occur. The bulk of the administrator's time with youngsters, however, will be spent in the two formerly mentioned manners of learning involvement and continued group guidance. From a guidance point of view, the Council and its further development will have the priority position. Gaining a positive status as regards the school's discipline problem level is not to be left unattended, however.

Originally the Council was to be labeled the Peace Council—their job being to help stop the fighting at Grant. However, it was felt by some staff members that at least for the present the name Council should be left alone without the adjective Peace. Seeing validity for the recommendation, the group is presently known as the Council—not, however, to be confused with some aspects of the Student Council concept. For example, it is felt at this time that parlimentary procedure seems more appropriate for a junior high school group or older.

The Grant School Council is a group of youngsters who help on the playground by reminding their peers of safety rules, who are called on to make suggestions for an improved school and who are called on to help around the school. This Council has been immeasurably helpful in reducing aggressive behavior at Grant. It has also greatly increased a positive school spirit. In her book, *Heal the Hurt Child*, Hertha Riese deals with how to help the neglected child. She says, "...it is of utmost importance to create an uplifting, inspiring group spirit...." [1]*. While the importance of a group or school spirit has always been known to be significant in the learning process, it is a frequently overlooked element in an elementary school. High schools, colleges and even junior high schools usually do well here, though sometimes from the limited platform of competitive sports.

It is significant to note by the way that though Dr. Riese's recommendation is for a school catering to youngsters from a neglected background, the recommendation holds good for all school or group situations. Furthermore, one should have the awareness that what a teacher does for the poor learners and those who are gifted together constitute sound educational

---

*See bibliography on page 221 for further information.

practice for all youngsters. Though this disposition is not a tested theory, there seems to be much supportive experience to indicate validity. Also, implied or meant to be implied in this theory is the importance of accepting as intrinsic the process of working with youngsters as individuals toward their developing a sense of self-worth. And, this major task can be accomplished by developing their talent(s), with academic success being perhaps but one avenue toward such a valued awareness.

Now, a few more clarifying statements about the Council before proceeding with the description of the next step taken at Grant—another step toward establishing the school's readiness for the implementation of such educational goals as suggested in the Learning Center philosophy.

The Council had 18 members—nine boys and nine girls. Six boys and six girls were elected from among their fourth- fifth- and sixth-grade peers and three of each sex were appointed by teacher recommendation to the principal. In a special school assembly, the Council members were "sworn in" to the task of loyally helping the youngsters of our school and the school as a whole. They were then presented with safety patrol belts (marked indelibly with a capital C) that they wore when on playground or hall duty. It may be interesting to note, that before the election for Council members was held, the youngsters were told that the "goody-goodies" need not be those elected. They were to elect those who were the leaders and who they believed would try to set a good example. (Some of the school's best known fighters were elected.)

Council membership has been sought after by many youngsters since its inception. A prime criterion for election is the demonstration of "improved" behavior. The word "im- proved" obviously is not meant to suggest arrival at a perfect state. Furthermore, it is an adjective to be applied to a youngster as an individual. Those elected are to be those concerned with the idea of improving and of being helpful to their schoolmates, teachers and school in general. At a recognition day assembly held for the first time in January, 1969, recognition was awarded the boy and the girl Council member who had most demonstrated the ideals of the Council.

The judging was done by their schoolmates and teachers, each with an equivalent voting power.

R-DAY (RECOGNITION DAY)

The biannual assembly has become an eventual tradition at Grant Elementary School. The idea of R-Day, like most of the ideas presented within the covers of this book, is not new. How it is to be done may be new, or at least some phases of it may be. Whether the idea is new or not, of course, is not important. What is important is its motivational efficacies—how it is used and how it may become a significant event in a planned set that together form a whole process—one that will implement a worthwhile educational philosophy.

Becoming evident here, perhaps, is that being mobilized is the greatest power source for the implementation of the finest of educational programs—the youngsters themselves. This idea in its dynamic dimension will be dealt with in Chapter 3 entitled "Preparing a Learning Center for Independent Study."

Educators have seldom been called upon to recognize the achievement of youngsters in terms other than A, B, C, D, and F, or E, S, U, or some such symbol system to indicate academic and attitude and effort levels. At Grant, however, and at other schools from time to time, a need was felt to recognize other kinds of successes, just as, if not more important, than the forms of achievement noted on report cards. R-Day was therefore instituted as the vehicle. It would be interesting for you the reader to list the behaviors you feel should be recognized, in priority order. For the fun of it, the author's list follows. If you wish you can cover up her list and make up your own, comparing and evaluating both of them. The author's list is not intended to be a fixed one nor could it be imagined that yours would be so either. How do we match up?

Recognition to be given at each grade level for the youngster who more than anyone else at this time:

1.	4.	7.	10.
2.	5.	8.	11.
3.	6.	9.	

The author's list for recognition to be given at each grade level for the youngster who more than anyone else at this time accomplished goals he had set for himself are:

1. Helps himself, his schoolmates and his school to improve.
2. Seems to enjoy school.
3. Has improved in working independently.
4. Chooses "smart" things to do to help himself learn.
5. Accepts a disappointment well.
6. Shows increased interest in new things to learn about.
7. Has developed more self-discipline.
8. Treats others more kindly and understandingly.
9. Has done much better in one or more academic areas.
10. Comes to school on time.
11. Has the best attendance record.

All deserving youngsters receive an award with the understanding that a goal is not a goal unless it is achievable. In addition, there are those students from each classroom who receive a special award for outstanding achievement by way of accomplishing especially challenging goals.

The first R-Day assembly was not run in the same way as it was later for a variety of reasons. The staff had decided that it would be a great deal of fun for the youngsters, and hopefully encouraging to them, to make the first assembly a surprise. Also, it was realized that improving the R-Day concept was a likelihood. And finally, it would be in the months ahead that more defining of the "worthwhile" behavior goals (several of which are Learning Center goals) would be done in the classrooms with the youngsters, so that as the assemblies progressed, we would have more success-oriented youngsters. And, as we know, success breeds a positive self-concept.

THE GRANT SCHOOL STAFF

It was mentioned earlier in this chapter that the Grant staff has become quite a fine group, and indeed they are. They have been quite supportive of the youngsters in many ways. They suggest ideas for better methods of accomplishing goals; they compliment Council members when they do a commendable job; they are enthusiastic about making youngsters happy in their learning process at school; they are eager to plan fun learning activities for the youngsters; they make changes (and sometimes uncomfortable ones for themselves) in order to better help their students. They also take the time to try to deal with children understandingly and give the principal ideas on how to do better, etc.

This fact of positive staff action could be greatly elaborated upon. However, let us simply consider what the Grant staff is really saying. By their deeds, by setting examples of cooperation and concern, they too are saying "we *care*" and their efforts are indeed having their effect. Grant School is really ready for a Learning Center because staff effort has established the kind of atmosphere conducive to Learning-Center implementation—an atmosphere that is an *absolute must* for Learning Center success.

A PTA SPEECH

Following is a speech I made at a PTA meeting. It is given here to show one more aspect of building a school's harmonious atmosphere, an atmosphere which is an absolute key to long-lasting Learning Center success (let alone the overall success of a school).

Good Evening and a warm welcome to Grant School. As always, I am delighted to be with you.

This evening I would like to formally report to you Grant School's progress this past year. During the course of last year, the staff, students and parents at Grant accomplished the following:

1. Through staff teamwork and the help of the Council of student helpers, they have improved the discipline and safety situation at Grant. There are fewer fights, fewer injured children and, very importantly, an apparently happier, more relaxed student body. This accomplishment is extremely important, for it is a key step to having a school that is ready to settle down and get down to the business of learning. This accomplishment is no small one and I, in fact, consider it crucial to establishing our school as one of the finest in Elgin, among the best in the state and, perhaps one day, outstanding in the country. Students need to feel proud of their school, that it is a good school where they can find fairness and understanding when they have a problem. We try very hard to bring this feeling to our youngsters at Grant, and I think if we had the time to ask each one of you here tonight if your youngster is perhaps a little happier in coming to school this year, a significant number of you would indeed reply "yes." If we have in fact accomplished that, then we have achieved the most important first step, a step without which your youngsters would learn little by comparison.

2. *Second*, and again through staff teamwork, we have set the goal for ourselves to let you know that we really *care* about your youngsters and that we really desire to get to know you better. In other words, we want *you*, the members of the Grant School community, to know that here is a school that is a *friendly* school, with people working here who want to reach out and work *with* you, to assure your youngsters of a happy and profitable school experience. There are those of you who may feel that you have reason to distrust us and may believe that we are trying to help some but not all members of our community. Those of you who feel that way, I'm asking you tonight to search within yourselves and see if you feel that I am standing here before you and not being honest. If after looking into yourselves you have any doubt about our good

intentions, then I am asking you right now to get rid of that doubt and spread the word to keep the faith. Grant School is working to do its best for *all* its children, and we wish and we hope that all of you will give us a welcome hand as we come out of this establishment to come into your homes and get to know you better. We would like to visit with you, to seek further ways of helping your children better and thereby know how to help them more. Though we may not be able to visit all the homes of all the families in the Grant School attendance area this year, that is our goal for the not too distant future. We do not want you to feel, however, that you have to have us over. We will only visit where we're invited.

3. *Third*, through the efforts of the P.T.A. and your school, available to you in the next couple of weeks for you to keep, is a Grant School Handbook. We urge you to read each and every page, for it contains much information that we think you'd like to know.

4. *Fourth*, Grant School has, as the result of organizational efforts made last year, a volunteer program which was set up with the help of Mrs. Ruth Brunton. A group of ten Elgin ladies are now working with the Grant School teachers to help your youngsters even more. Many of these volunteers serve as teacher's aides. The reports I have received both from the youngsters and teachers indicate that the help of these volunteers is much welcomed and appreciated.

5. *Fifth*, we now have the kinds of materials in our Learning Center that are especially designed to aid the teacher in helping each youngster learn as an individual. Several teachers are already using our Learning Center to head in the direction of individualizing instruction, which I can assure you is a most dedicated direction to take.

The foregoing accomplishments are no small or easy ones. Each teacher sitting in this room literally spends hours and hours of extra time with the conviction that doing the best is but the least that we can do.

It is at this point that I would like to make a special request of each of you parents, and if

you would, I'd appreciate your spreading the word
to those who were unable to be here tonight. Let
these teachers know, let me know, let others
know whenever you think your youngster's
teacher has done something that you think is
"good." While we generally hear your concerns,
and that is as it should be, we don't always hear
your words of praise. As I said, this may sound
like an unusual request, but there isn't a one of us
here tonight who does not appreciate being told
about something good they have done. Kind
words really help and spur us all on to do even
bigger and better things for your children—and
speaking of your children, it is also important
that you let them know when you think their
teacher is doing something great. Your child's respect for his teacher will increase if you set the
example, and that is, of course, important. So let
us hear your concerns, but very importantly too,
let us also hear your words of praise. By the way,
I think I know someone else whom I think would
enjoy hearing the good things and that is the superintendent of our district—Dr. Paul Lawrence.
He is a fine man who makes many of these good
things possible.

Before closing, I would like to introduce to
you a Mr. Wendel Sharpe. Mr. Sharpe has taught
several years and is presently working on his
master's degree in elementary school guidance at
Northern Illinois University. Two days each week,
Mr. Sharpe is assigned to Grant School to further
help our students understand their problems so
that your children can do even better in school. If
he should have the opportunity to call on you, I
know you'll be as impressed with this young man
and his concern and knowledge of how to help
children as we are.

It is now that time of the evening when
you'll be hearing from your youngsters' teachers
about their plans for their class this year. I suggest
that husbands go to one of their youngsters'
rooms and the wives to another, in an effort to
gain the most information. When the teacher is
through with his or her presentation you may
wish to ask questions, but we ask that you do not

try to talk to the teacher about your child. We consider it unprofessional to hold a conference publicly. Do feel free, however, to invite your youngsters' teachers over to your home, if you so desire, or feel free to request a conference one day here at school. Also, in about a half hour from now you will hear a bell. That'll be our way of saying we've enjoyed being with you, but it's time to go. In closing, I want to urge you again to feel free to call on me here at school. I am never too busy to see what I can do to be of help, for I feel that people, much more so than my paper work, are my business.

3

Preparing a Learning Center
for Independent Study

Developing a workable Learning Center for independent study requires much planning and teamwork by the school's staff. Without the commitment and direct involvement of the whole staff or at least a majority, the program will be shallow and probably more for public relations than for the genuine benefit of all the youngsters of a school.

Once a staff is committed to the *idea* of a Learning Center—more even than the establishment of a place called a Learning Center—the second most important consideration is *who* gets to use the place and why. It is obvious that the gifted youngsters would benefit from an independent study facility, but the underachievers do well too. Remediation needs are served. Behavior-problem youngsters, and the very difficult ones too, do just fine. Teachers have found it fun to follow along on interest study projects. Nonreaders from second grade on up find their way. Mature first graders manage quite nicely. (And how about parents and grandparents, too?) The philosophy certainly indicates

51

that *all* can be involved. Experience unquestioningly says this too. In fact, it's a must that all be involved if for no other reason than from a motivational standpoint. Tell someone they can accomplish good independent study habits, give them a structure, guidance and encouragement—and they can. Tell them they can't, even just for now, and they won't. The teacher who when contemplating an independent study program for her students says "yes, but" is frequently either an autocratic, authoritarian type and/or one who cannot comfortably handle groups of youngsters. Too many administrators and teachers of this ilk have dampened, modified to the deadly point or completely overruled coping with the challenge of progress, and in particular the challenge of freeing youngsters to think and learn for themsleves. Basically they are threatened by the thought that if they attempt something different they might not know how. Perhaps the attitude to assume then is: yes, we'll goof some things up—maybe even a lot of things—but so what? We'll backtrack, or regear, rethink or whatever else is necessary to achieve our goals. It has been done and if "they" can, *we* can! In fact, all that is required to succeed is simply an enthusiastic appreciation of Learning Center goals, group effort and thorough, ongoing involvement and evaluation. Oh yes, some money also helps.

The third major consideration is how much time shall a youngster be able to spend studying independently? A logical reply could be "100 percent!" This question perhaps requires no exact reply. More important than the maximum is the minimum amount of time each youngster should spend. A minimum for all youngsters would be 5 per cent of a week's time in school. A sample Learning Center schedule, providing the youngsters of a school a minimum of two hours per week for second grade on up and one hour per week to begin with for the first graders, can be found in Chapter 9; kindergartners can also be scheduled for book exchange and a story time each week. By the way, it's a good idea to pull from the book return cart 50 or so primary level books and spread them out on a group of tables. Then the youngsters can pick out the book they want much more easily than by choosing from the stacks.

This job should be done about 15 minutes before the little ones arrive.

Once the *minimum* time is provided, the goal is then to help each youngster be able to attain the possible ultimate—the hypothetical 100 per cent.

THE STATIONS CONCEPT

The Stations concept is worthwhile to consider when planning for a Learning Center. It is meant to signify a school that contains a variety of facilities designed for certain purposes. They are to be under the leadership of a regular classroom teacher who is responsible for that facility as a resource person, having a background appropriate to the purpose of the facility. The teacher would not be solely in charge of what happened with her facility, however. The principal and staff would play their part through cooperative decision making. The resource teacher would then be the organizer and responsible agent. When hiring personnel with this concept in mind, it is important to be sure that, while you want teachers with a specialty, nonetheless, these teachers should be child oriented rather than subject oriented. (Need we illustrate this point more vividly than by bringing to mind the tragedy of our subject-oriented, ability-grouping type junior high schools?)

Areas for specialty could be:

a. drama

b. physical education

c. speech therapy

d. languages

e. dancing

f. arts and crafts

g. library

h. preschool

i. guidance

j. learning disability

k. social studies

l. science

m. reading

n. math

o. inquiry training

p. kindergarten

q. group dynamics

The stations might include:

a. Little theatre (doubling as a science seminar room).

b. Gyms and playground.

c. Office areas.

d. Classroom(s), housing appropriate materials for teaching English as a second language if such is more feasible than housing such materials in the Learning Center.

e. Records and a record player housed in the gym for dancing.

f. All materials for arts and crafts located in the studios—see Figure 6-6, Chapter 6.

g. The library resources teacher's (not to be confused with the "traditional" librarian) station could be a classroom that has a mobile cart containing materials with which to instruct all youngsters in library science—it is easier to instruct in the classroom and besides, the Learning Center is for independent study.

h. Preschool living rooms and play areas should be provided when building a new school. See Figure 6-5, Chapter 6.

i. There should be guidance facilities in every school. See Figure 6-5, Chapter 6. The person needed for this station would be full time and a certified guidance counselor.

j. First-grade classrooms equipped to work with learning-disability youngsters. One of the first-grade teachers should be qualified by the state for learning-disability work. The office area may serve for small-group instruction. See Figure 6-5, Chapter 6.

k, l, m, n. One classroom per grade-level cluster or per two grade-level clusters, equipped for the skill subjects mentioned previously in the areas-for-specialty list. Some independent study activities could be housed in the Center and some in the resource rooms, as well as the needed materials of course being located in these places.

o. Investigate inquiry training for youngsters and provide some primary and intermediate classrooms with materials such as Suchman's.

Perhaps it would be well at this point to mention that the ungraded concept is not tenable when the result is ability grouping or tracking. Ability grouping and tracking, one of the prominent outcomes of ungradedness, is a negative outcome. Independent study and individualized instruction (with high teacher-expected student achievement) is much more the answer, particularly SPI as described in Chapter 4. Graded classrooms are just fine, based upon maturity promotion at the kindergarten level with heterogeneous grouping and independent study. Another direction to take is the family grouping idea as developed in the British schools.

At Grant Elementary School in Elgin a form of the British primary school concept is being employed, so that by the time a youngster reaches second grade he is going on with the ability to at least achieve at grade level. EMH and learning disability youngsters are identified by observation and testing in kindergarten and are provided for by the next year. In other words, at Grant, a program has been established to make sure that each youngster will achieve at least average academic success from second grade on without being assigned to any "slow" group—a very damaging assignment.

Perhaps it can now be seen that the Stations concept and gradedness is meant to imply that the whole schoolhouse is to be thought of as a Learning Center and without the noise and confusion that inevitably result from trying to build a practically wall-less interior to a school, such as Scheme 3, Figure 6-4 in Chapter 6 indicates. Too many people in education who are in earnest, and desire the worthwhile goal of having the whole school be a Learning Center, gloss over the noise aspect of a wall-less though acoustically defined school, saying that youngsters can work just fine in noise or at least in an environment where sound is kept at the low roar level. A more capable student can block out sound effectively. Studies indicate, however, that the slow student cannot work when surrounded by noise. He is too easily distracted. But why bother trying to push for a one-room schoolhouse to house about 700 students just because it sounds good? More at issue and more importantly, do we want our youngsters to have more noise in their lives? Young adults at age 25 today are already becoming hard of hearing from the high volume level of their society. Furthermore, youngsters who come from large families often have a difficult time finding a quiet corner. What about them? And, where do we learn to enjoy peace and contentment through quietness? Where do we learn the value of quiet? We already know that keeping a high volume level is a method of escaping from self. Thus, if our key goal is to help each individual achieve a positive self-view, then we would be defeating our main purpose by allowing the merchants of noise for our schools to woo us into agreeing it into existence.

What is being advocated then is the combining and acquiring of learning aids and specific know-how to achieve the sort of goals described as Learning Center goals in Chapter 1. The kind of change required to accomplish these goals is more a change of focus for our schools rather than completely altered, unrecognizably different school facilities, though ones that can promote learning. These changes demand different teacher behaviors for many teachers and for others a low bow, because they've already been accomplishing such goals. The greatest threat to change as was alluded to earlier is a fear of failure. We need not fail.

In conclusion here, the Stations concept seems a most likely modus operandi, therefore, for a Learning Center concept, meaning the whole of a school rather than one or two rooms of a school. It, or a better method, seems worthy of implementation. Let it not be implied, however, that primary or lower intermediate grade levels are to be departmentalized. Minimum departmentalization is recommended as a rule of thumb.

A LOOK AT WHAT YOU HAVE AND WHAT YOU WANT

Problem solving, goal setting and positive-type staff interaction is absolutely necessary in order to use an existing school facility to its fullest. It would be well at this point to describe more of the particulars involved in establishing an old building such as Grant to illustrate what can be done.

FIGURE 3-1: Left Section Built 1882; Middle Section Built 1900; Right Section Built 1911 (Grant School).

Grant School was built in stages. The original structure was completed in 1882. Somewhere between 1882 and 1911, an addition was put on. In 1911, the final or third section of the building was completed. In the picture of Grant, you will be able to note these stages of growth. The rooms at Grant are generally large and have high ceilings. There are 17 different stair levels and several interesting, useful nooks and crannies— one of the beauties of an old building. It's the kind of place that grows on you and you come to love. It is the kind of building that is just fine for developing the whole school Learning Center concept.

FIGURE 3—2: Grant School's Learning Center B.

Before reading on, take a moment to look over the pictures of the inside of Grant School. Upstairs, in the middle of the hall, several of the independent study materials, the magazine rack and the nonfiction section of the school's library are located. Fiction books are housed in each classroom. The hall #2 nook or Learning Center B contains more independent study materials. Times are established for the sharing of all materials. Youngsters in small groups may use the materials in a classroom other than their own at any given time, whenever the need or a student's interest indicates this action.

By the way, youngsters have been known to misbehave in order to be free to work on their own. They had teachers who used the Center area for punishment and as a dumping ground for their discipline problems—an unfortunate policy to be scrupulously avoided. It is up to the administrator and staff to work out a positive alternative when a youngster needs to be removed temporarily from his classroom. The form in Figure 3—4 is to be implemented at Grant this year as a procedural guide. Its use would precede a youngster being sent to the office when the need arises for him to be separated from the class setting. Whether or not the procedure it indicates will be the same by the end of the year as at the beginning remains to be seen.

ORGANIZING THE MATERIALS

Each classroom at Grant has its own little library, primarily of fiction storybooks. To say that Grant must have an addition built, in order to house these books and other materials centrally, seems a more expensive recommendation than it's worth. It is important, nonetheless, that there be access to these books and other learning tools. To be undertaken, therefore, is an extension of the teaming concept. By providing

FIGURE 3—3: Grant School's Learning Center A.

GRANT ELEMENTARY SCHOOL
Elgin, Illinois

CONFIDENTIAL REFERRAL FORM
(to be done in duplicate)

_____ indicates a need for our concern because (s)he has a (health-social-emotional-academic-discipline-tardy-absenteeism-other) (circle applicable word or words) problem. Description:

_____

_____

(Continue with cum folder information on reverse side)

Date_____

STEPS TAKEN
(Give dates for each occurrence)

1. Private conference with youngster: _____

_____

2. Home visitation to say "hello" (get acquainted) _____

_____

3. Home visitations and/or phone calls to discuss "problem" . . . give dates and parental reaction:

_____

_____

4. The family would benefit from a social worker's (district and/or community) service _____ yes _____ no.

5. Problem referred to Principal _____
   Date

Principal's Action:

(Additional commentary on other side: _____ yes _____ no)

FIGURE 3–4

Teacher's Name   Grade   Phone Number   Room Number   Age   First and Last Name of Student times for youngsters to go to any classroom in the building to borrow and later return what they would like to use, the whole building then becomes the Center and each classroom a learning station—some of which may be designated for quiet study and others for group study. Another way to proceed, particularly in a larger building, would be to team at the primary level, when primary classrooms as a group are opened up, and at the intermediate level or by any method that evolves and works in your building.

Now that we have the students in motion, how do they find what they're interested in? Here's where a simplified card cataloging system comes in handy. The cards would indicate where—in what room, or hall, or closet the materials are located. This information can easily be added to the sets of cards purchased with each book. There would probably be at least two quite accessible card catalogs, identical in composition—not a "primary" one indicating "primary" located materials but a total building catalog. It would also be recommended that the card catalog have:

    a. Author cards for fiction books only.

    b. Title cards for biographies, fiction books, fiction filmstrips and independent study materials of the sort listed in Chapter 6.

    c. Subject cards for nonfiction books, independent study materials, nonfiction filmstrips, nonfiction vertical file materials, nonfiction shortstrips, nonfiction films and nonfiction study prints.

The foregoing recommendation is not seen to be imperative but would seem easier for the youngsters as well as less work for the clerks (or volunteers), especially when cards have to be made up for each book and each material, as is the case at Grant. What is important to keep in mind when considering this procedure is that it does not actually change the established system. Rather it simplifies it. Furthermore, the modification is consistent with the full-blown system, and in library science consistency is a key concept.

See Figures 3-5, 3-6, 3-7, and 3-8 on pages 63-66 for

sample cards. Please note that none of the nonfiction material or book cards contain subnumerations or fractionalizations. This procedure is recommended for elementary and perhaps even junior high schools.

ORGANIZING THE OPERATION OF A LEARNING CENTER

Once the staff has decided on the starting goals for their Learning Center, organized their materials, hired any auxiliary personnel (if possible at least a clerk), taught themselves the operation of the materials and made the goal cards, they are ready to begin.

STEP 1 — Decide which classes shall begin—generally the older ones first. Keep the number beginning to a maximum of four classes. Each day or each week, more can be added as the "bugs" are worked out of the system.

STEP 2 — Spend two to three separate occasions with each class, establishing the following values:

a. it is smart to select the appropriate material for yourself—some anecdotes to the effect that we are not fooled when someone's pretending he can do something he actually can't. If it's too easy, you won't learn. If it's too hard, you won't learn either. Plus you'll be bored using a material that is not right for you.

b. it is a privilege to have the opportunity of choosing those materials and/or projects you'd like to work on (a privilege not to be taken away for misbehavior).

c. it is smart to take advantage of the opportunity of this extra time to improve in a subject area, or to get ahead in a subject area. (By lesson planning broadly a month ahead of time and posting these plans, the youngsters can and frequently do choose to advance their knowledge of a unit and thereby have the opportunity to gain recognition in a positive fashion.)

NOTE: The format for these cards is simple. The nonfiction number is probably not accurate but does illustrate form, nonetheless. All names and titles used are meant to be fictitious. Color coding the general nonfiction classifications would be ideal. Example: all animal books have a pink tab on the spine and a pink tab on the card-catalog card.

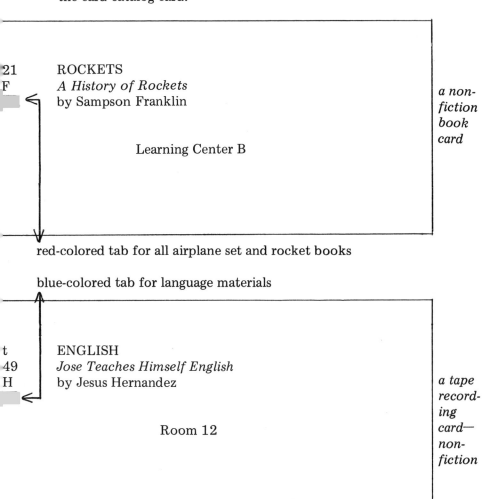

21
F

ROCKETS
A History of Rockets
by Sampson Franklin

Learning Center B

a non-fiction book card

red-colored tab for all airplane set and rocket books

blue-colored tab for language materials

t
49
H

ENGLISH
Jose Teaches Himself English
by Jesus Hernandez

Room 12

a tape record-ing card— non-fiction

FIGURE 3–5

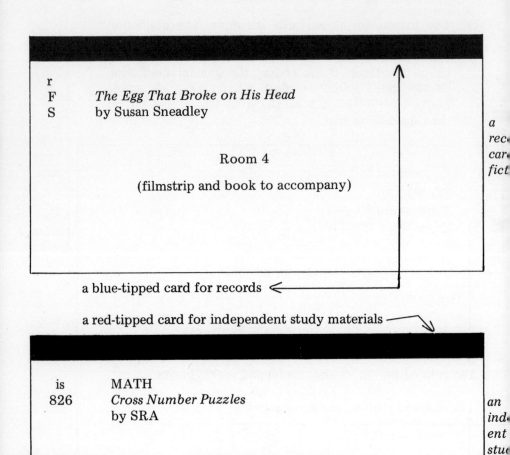

r
F   *The Egg That Broke on His Head*
S   by Susan Sneadley

Room 4

(filmstrip and book to accompany)

a
rec
car
fict

a blue-tipped card for records ⟵

a red-tipped card for independent study materials

is   MATH
826   *Cross Number Puzzles*
          by SRA

Learning Center A

an
ind
ent
stu
ma
car

FIGURE 3-6

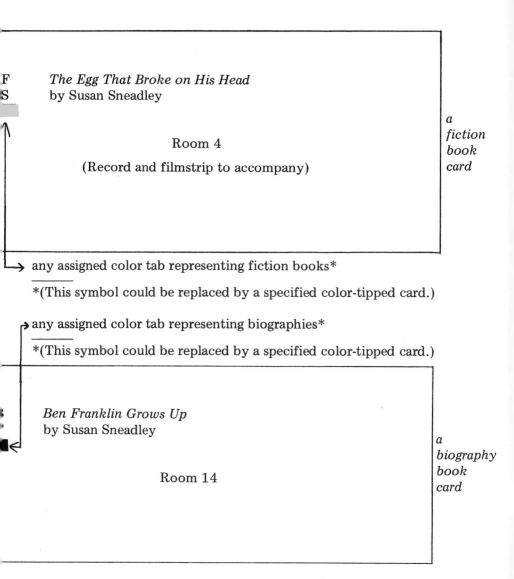

F
S

The Egg That Broke on His Head
by Susan Sneadley

Room 4

(Record and filmstrip to accompany)

*a
fiction
book
card*

any assigned color tab representing fiction books*

*(This symbol could be replaced by a specified color-tipped card.)

any assigned color tab representing biographies*

*(This symbol could be replaced by a specified color-tipped card.)

Ben Franklin Grows Up
by Susan Sneadley

Room 14

*a
biography
book
card*

FIGURE 3-7

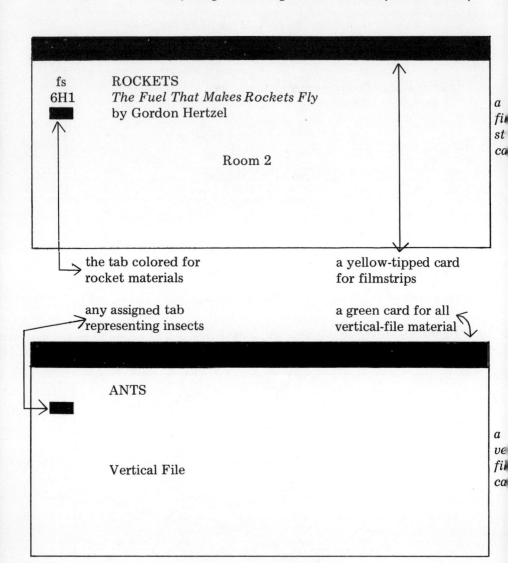

fs
6H1

ROCKETS
The Fuel That Makes Rockets Fly
by Gordon Hertzel

Room 2

*a
fi
st
ca*

the tab colored for
rocket materials

a yellow-tipped card
for filmstrips

any assigned tab
representing insects

a green card for all
vertical-file material

ANTS

Vertical File

*a
ve
fi
ca*

FIGURE 3-8

    d. it is smart to keep track of where you've left off from day to day on your goal card calendar. A sample notation might be PL, IIa, Bk 6, p. 12, which means: Pilot Library, kit IIa, Book 6, page 12. Some reasons for getting into the habit are that it helps you remember where you left off and it helps to evaluate your progress.

    e. it is smart to work neatly, for neat work means more correct work. Neat work on a final product is a must to stress, for it is a reflection of how a youngster feels about himself.

    f. it is often helpful to use the answer sheets to learn by.

    g. it is dumb to waste time by cheating, and the youngster won't accomplish the goal he, himself, set if he does—plus it's boring to cheat. The ultimate decision for this is in the hands of the youngster, however. A teacher could say something to this effect, "It is easy to fool me if you want to cheat, but how about yourself or your friends?"

    h. it is fun to be your own boss.

    i. it is fun to have an interest study.

    j. it is fun to improve.

    k. it is fun to help others learn.

STEP 3 — Make sure the youngsters understand what a goal is, what it means to have a goal and what it means to improve. Goals are for everyone and everyone needs to improve. There is always more to learn.

STEP 4 — Pass out a goal card to each youngster. Have them put their name and room number on it. Then tell them that if they know what their goals are, they can fill in the appropriate blanks at the top. Some, but not many youngsters, take about a month to decide. Pass out construction paper to each child (18" x 24") to make Learning Center folders.

STEP 5 — Youngsters go to the Learning Center with their teacher to determine which materials will be the ones they want to work with. You may wish to set a rule that when they mark their decisions for what materials they wish to use on their goal cards they are committed to these materials for a month. Urge them, therefore, to decide carefully. In fact it's wise if they try it out first and then make a decision. It has been absolutely thrilling to me on certain occasions when a youngster has come up on his own and said, "Miss Glasser, I tried this level of SRA and it's too hard for me... I think I'll try the next level down." What a joy to reply "Yes, son, that sounds like a wise decision."

STEP 6 — Youngsters find the place they wish to work.

STEP 7 — Make sure the youngsters understand which are the quiet working areas and which are for group work. At Grant School, the youngsters made this decision of which area was to be which. (An anecdote at this point seems fitting. Imagine a classroom filled with youngsters working quietly in a room they designated as a Quiet Room, engrossed with materials of their choice, and a fun-loving youngster, needing attention, felt like clowning. This youngster leaned over to another and began to create a disturbance. In unison, his classmates turned around and said "sh..." Meekly, quietly, the boy returned to his work.) It's frequent occasions such as this one when you know that when youngsters are really given the responsibility for their own learning... wow it's beautiful, and the younger, the sooner, the better. It's not always easy, especially when there are those youngsters who will push to see if you really mean what you say. Nonetheless, stand pat. The youngsters are not and, in fact, *never* are "wasting" the "free" Learning Center time. They are testing, experiencing and experimenting. The most significant rule being, and justifiably imposed, is that it is not fair to disturb others during their exploratory period.

STEP 8 — Keep an eye out for those youngsters who seem to be floundering. They need your guidance, encouragement and support. They are not simply fooling around, even if it appears so. Remember—those who can, do. Those who can't need your help to learn how.

STEP 9 — Meet with the other teachers thus far involved, to work out the problems and list recommendations for the next groups to join the Learning Center program.

STEP 10 — Team up to help the teachers not already involved with their classes during their Learning Center times if possible.

STEP 11 — Evaluate. Keep an ongoing dialog going between all (including youngsters) involved. Try to get used to having what seems like a good idea . . . bomb.

STEP 12 — Establish a method to allow one-to-one conferences between each teacher and each of her students. Useful for conferencing could be something like the Pupil-Teacher Learning Center Conference Guide and Record Sheet Figure 3—9. The teacher would be supplied a three-ring loose-leaf notebook and about 50 of these forms and perhaps index separators. It is a must to make sure in a methodical manner that each youngster is getting whatever guidance he requires to function well and enjoy working independently. If in conferencing with a youngster he

_____
Pupil's Last Name

Pupil—Teacher
Learning Center
Conference Guide
and
Record Sheet

1. From your experience in the past, what have you learned that would help set better goals for yourself?

2. What projects, activities, subjects would you like to learn more about?

_____   _____   _____

_____   _____   _____

3. What do you want the Learning Center to provide or do for you this year?

_____

_____

4. What materials were most helpful to you?

| *PROJECT* | *BEST MATERIALS* |

a. Title:_____
    date:_____

b. Title:_____
    date:_____

c. Title:_____
    date:_____

d. Title:_____
    date:_____

e. Title:_____
    date:_____

f. Title:_____
    date:_____

FIGURE 3-9

FOR Teacher Use:

PROGRESS RECORD

(Place a yes or no in each box)	OCT.	FEB.	MAY
1. Can work 2 hours/week independently.			
2. Can work 4 hours/week independently.			
3. Can work 8 hours/week independently.			
4. Can complete a self-assigned project.			
5. Can complete a teacher-assigned project.			
6. Enjoys working independently.			
7. Can functionally use:			
(a) Card catalog			
(b) Independent study materials			
(c) Filmstrips			
(d) All A-V equipment			
(e) Encyclopedias			
(f) Dictionary			
(g) Magazine reference guides			
(h) Vertical file			

FIGURE 3-9, Continued

seems aimless and phlegmatic, it might help to have available the Attitude Survey. See Chapter 8.

STEP 13 — Train the youngsters to keep track of their pleasure reading. See Figure 3-10.

MY READING RECORD
RIDGE SCHOOL 1967-1968

TITLE	AUTHOR	Kind of book: *E*asy Fiction, or *F*iction, or *N*onfiction (number of book) or *B*iography	I might like to read this book again. Yes	I would not like to read this book again. No

FIGURE 3-10

SUGGESTIONS FOR SOME INDEPENDENT INTEREST STUDY PROJECTS

1. Design a model automobile or truck.
2. Read about how comic strips (cartoons) are done—then create your own.
3. Draw, color, label and tell about (or write about) a rocket.
4. Read about map making and draw to scale the school grounds.

5. Find out how to measure the height of our school's flagpole without climbing it.

6. Write your own biography about a favorite composer, artist, mathematician.

7. Make an outline of the important developments of your favorite city—you can make a time line chart to go with it.

8. Find out why the people of Egypt live where they do. How many reasons can you find?

9. How many different facts can you write down about the Mississippi River?

10. Read the book *Women of Courage!* How did each woman show courage? What is **your** definition of courage?

11. Make a list of as many **different** kinds of conservation that you can think of by reading.

12. Make a list of the improvements made on the American rifle.

13. Read three easy books on the same subject. Write a report telling what **new** things you've learned about the subject from **each** book.

14. Same as above except with three nonfiction books.

15. Find ten books about automobiles. Write their titles on a piece of paper. Underline the titles of the books that have the **best** pictures in them.

16. Can you, without asking anyone, find out the ten longest rivers of the world? How many nonfiction books do we have about them? Pick three to read and report on.

17. What does the word "archeology" mean? Read the book on reserve.

18. If you want to play teacher after school, then why don't you make a list of questions to ask your friends, about the United States?

19. Make a diorama about birds.

20. Write your own little book about dinosaurs. Illustrate it, too.

21. Learn about the Incas and teach Mrs. Smith's class about it. Draw pictures, write notes, put on a little play to illustrate.

22. Get a group together with a common interest and put on a play.

23. Find out about the history of dolls. Could you draw several to show the differences in how they're made?

24. Why did the *Titanic* sink?

A PRIMARY LEVEL LEARNING CENTER PROGRAM – ONE IDEA

Successfully implemented at the Brentwood School, District 59, Illinois, was a primary level interest study program. The teachers grouped their youngsters in threes and fours according to similar learning interests. Taken into consideration too, was setting up these groups to enhance the social development of the youngsters involved. Some of the groups wanted to study fossils, others cats, still others eggs hatching, baseball, sports in general, flowers, volcanoes, electricity, engines, etc. Then, older youngsters were asked to volunteer to lead these groups—youngsters who had learning interests in common. While the groups were primarily arranged according to sex—a male group with a male leader (usually dictated because of the interests held in common)—nonetheless, there were groups that operated successfully with a leader of the opposite sex.

The upper-grade leaders were released from their classes through an arrangement worked out to help them make up work with their teacher's or classmates' help. They were released during the Learning Center assigned times of their primary group. Neither scholastic standing nor good behavior were criteria permitting youngsters to become leaders. As it worked out, it was indeed a positive fun experience for all involved—even for those upper graders you'd think couldn't afford to miss their classwork—and they were usually the first to volunteer. Frequently, these same youngsters seem to benefit the most in terms of ego boost and desire to learn. Therefore, if you want to have the fun of watching eager little tykes awaiting their leaders and conscientious pupils preparing to be good leaders, try this program.

One more thing. If you undertake this plan, arrange meetings with the leaders that are geared to enabling their success. They have the same problems teachers do. What do I do with a goof-off? What do I do with someone who doesn't want to join in? What do I suggest as interesting projects for the youngsters to do? These meetings can be conducted by the Learning Center teacher if there is one, by the principal or by an interested teacher.

A SUGGESTED LIST OF READINGS

Allan, James W. "Sooner Than You Think," *California School Libraries*, 39: 112-114 (March, 1968).

American Library Association and National Education Association. *Standards for School Media Programs*. Chicago: American Library Association, 1969.

Billings, Jane. "Selecting for the Instructional Materials Center," *Wisconsin Library Bulletin*, 64: 9-12 (January, 1968).

Brandt, Madeline, "Library Is a Learning Laboratory," *California School Libraries*, 38: 17 (November, 1966).

Darling, Richard C. "A Bit Beyond Promise," *School Library Journal*, 15: 23-26 (November, 1968).

Estes, Nolan. "Educational Excellence: An End to Cultural Isolation," *ALA Bulletin*, 63: 221-225 (February, 1969).

Gaver, Mary. *Effectiveness of Centralized Library Service in Elementary Schools*, 2nd ed. New Brunswick, N.J.: Rutgers University Press, 1963.

Gaver, Mary. *Patterns of Development in Elementary School Libraries Today*, 2nd ed. New York: Encyclopedia Britannica, 1965.

Gottesman, Alexander M. "Education in the Seventies," *Peabody Journal of Education*, 45: 76-81 (July, 1967).

"Instructional Materials-Libraries," *Illinois Journal of Education* (September, 1968).

Kremple, Frederick A. "Integrating Libraries into Learning Resources," *Catholic Library World*, 39: 470-480 (March, 1968).

Knight, Hattie and Elsie Adams. "The Instructional Materials Center Concept," *Peabody Journal of Education*, 45:303-305 (March, 1968).

Library Journal, 93: 256 (January 15, 1968).

Lowrie, Jan E. "Organization and Operation of School Libraries," *Library Trends*, 16: 211-227 (October, 1967).

Mahar, Mary H., ed. *The School Library as a Materials Center*. Washington: U.S. Government Printing Office, 1963.

Miller, Marjorie. "The Development of an Instructional Materials Center," *Illinois Libraries*, 50: 938-943 (November, 1968).

Porter, David S. "How to Design a Working Instructional Materials Center," *Educational Screen and Audio-Visual Guide*, 46: 23-25 (November, 1967).

Shellen, Rev. John J. "The Instructional Materials Center—Roma Nostra," *Catholic Library World*, 39: 412-413 (February, 1968).

Sleeman, Phillip J. and Robert Goff. "The Instructional Materials Center: Dialogue or Discord?" *AV Communication Review*, 15: 160-168 (Summer, 1967).

Srygley, Sara K. "Role and Function of the Elementary School Library," *Elementary English*, 44: 472-474 (May, 1967).

Sullivan, Peggy. *Impact: The School Library and the Instructional Program. A Report on Phase I of the Knapp School Libraries Project*. Chicago: American Library Association, 1967.

Taylor, Kenneth I. "The Instructional Materials Center:

A Theory Underlying Its Development," *Wisconsin Library Bulletin*, 63: 289-294 (September, 1967).

Taylor, Kenneth I. "The School System Instructional Materials Program: Evolving Maturity and Curriculum Support," *Wisconsin Library Bulletin*, 64: 331-335 (September, 1968).

Whitenack, Carolyn I. "School Libraries — School Media Centers," *ALA Bulletin*, 63: 249-266 (February, 1969).

Williamson, Walter W. "Developing an Instructional Materials Center in the Mount Royal School," *Educational Leadership*, 25: 167 (November, 1967).

AN IMPLEMENTATION CHECKLIST

The following checklist was developed to establish, in priority order, what needs to transpire in order to establish a workable, growing Learning Center.

— Receive district sanction and encouragement.

— Develop or embellish a wholesome school climate. Construct behavior perimeters for students and staff, involving the students in their guidelines and the staff in theirs—both together.

— Study what has been done with Learning Centers.

— Develop a building's Learning Center goals with staff and students, based upon your school's uniqueness as well as desirable universal type goals.

— Call for a voluntary staff Learning Center committee.

— Through group process establish some initial duties and responsibilities.

— Designate central housing areas for materials—hallway, classroom, library, building addition or rolling carts where necessary and helpful. Classrooms may be used as learning labs on a scheduled basis.

— Inventory and utilize present materials.

— Buy materials that lend themselves to the interests of youngsters, the skill development of youngsters and to independent as well as assigned study.

— Hire one librarian per 3,000 children. In other words, she could serve five schools with approximately 600 students per building. She would be a consultant to the staffs of each building, *advise* on material purchases, order materials and generally supervise the *organization* and the clerk's tasks of each school's Learning Center.

— Establish a simple but consistent card catalog system.

— Train teachers in operation of materials.

— Designate a group, a heterogeneous one, to pilot Learning Center implementation. Work out "bugs" in system.

— Set up new operational guidelines to improve system.

— Evaluate. Get more groups going.

— Expand program.

— Set up ongoing evaluative procedures.

— Organize parent volunteer worker group. Make schedule. Develop parent talent resource pool.

4

Encouraging Independent

vs.

Dependent Relationships

I n establishing a Learning Center, a key decision to be reached by the leadership involved is whether or not they are committed to "freeing" children. Do we wish to continue the teacher-instructor, pupil-listener type role or establish a revised teacher role—that of training and guiding youngsters from elementary school age on up, teaching them how to work well independently and how to make sound learning decisions for themselves? While this approach does not preclude students working in Centers on teacher-assigned projects, nonetheless, it does imply as a key raison d'être training youngsters in materials operation and appropriate selection to meet their own learning needs and/or their own defined learning goals. This opportunity also implies, by the way, that a part of a school's function is to train youngsters to meet the realities of life. For example, it is well known that an element of living a happy life is being able to make decisions for oneself and from self-determined goals. In fact, this skill is crucial and is often lacking in too many adults. Here, therefore, would be a major and ongoing experience early in the youngsters' lives, where they are guided in how to make decisions and in defining what ingredients (primarily meaningful goals) are necessary in employing that ability.

It is further contended and shown by experience that when independent rather that dependent student behavior is encouraged, a more comprehensive use is made of materials. They do not collect dust upon the shelf. Another result is that the students become involved in evaluating materials, and this involvement deepens a youngster's sense of responsibility regarding his use of the Learning Center. Speaking of responsibility, another key element of living happily and successfully is being able to accept the fact that "I," as an individual, am responsible for everything I do. If anything goes wrong or doesn't work out, "I" am to blame—not my environment, not my parents, not my crippled leg, not any other type of rationalization. Conversely, if "I" do something well, "I" may take the full credit. We want to train children to be able to accept this kind of responsibility rather than be frightened away from the comfort that its acceptance does indeed bring.

SELF-PRESCRIBED INSTRUCTION

At a commencement from undergraduate school ceremony a speaker said, in effect, if you are now capable of studying on your own, we here have indeed done our job.

While working at the graduate level, we were told that we were being prepared to conduct research projects and how to communicate our findings accurately. It seemed obvious when reflecting upon these goals, that even if a student were thusly capable, this training and much of his elementary and high school years of study could well be wasted. Motivation, stemming from a pleasure in learning, semed to be crucial as an added factor before such lofty goals as the above-stated ones would be worth the effort. How to make learning an exciting quest became, therefore, a driving ambition because as a goal it made just as much sense for elementary school youngsters to have the fun of learning independently as college graduates. The opportunity to so motivate elementary level youngsters arrived when it became the task to define what a Learning Center is and how to run one while at the Brentwood and Ridge schools in Elk Grove.

In those early days at Brentwood, the explanation given of a Learning Center's function seemed little more than a type of classroom operation. The youngsters were tested in reading and math, were assigned a specific material based on the results of the tests and were told to spend their time in the Learning Center doing something like starting in SRA Lab IIa and possibly ending there—whether they enjoyed it or not, whether they were bored or not. Empathetic directors added an important dimension—they gave some selection opportunities to the children. This type of operation was still rather depressing, however.

MOTIVATION AND SPI

How to motivate children to enjoy learning? How to do this systematically for a whole school? Those were especially agonizing questions for me to answer while standing in the midst of a lovely carpeted, well-organized and supplied Learning Center. Interest study became the first and later the most enduring and meaningful answer. The second solution, an extension of the above form of self-prescribed learning, became self-prescribed instruction using the paper-and-pencil type materials or newly developed machine-oriented programs (as described in Chapter 6).

Of the two solutions to motivation mentioned in the foregoing paragraph, it was more difficult to answer a child's question of "Why should I?" in terms of the first, namely interest study. "Because it's fun" was certainly one obvious answer but the "what should I do with it?" aspect of the question "why?" surfaced as the more challenging. Evolving from this challenge came the really not new concept of projects—an interest study project to share with classmates, to be a teacher's aide, to lead a discussion group, to make books for the library and for children's hospitals, etc. Learning thus found real purpose, much as your reading this book is learning with a purpose.

The ultimate in learning was the next step, to cultivate the habit of learning for the sheer joy of it—learning for the sake of learning—the satisfaction of a demanding curiosity. Studies meaningful to each individual youngster is perhaps the only or certainly the key way.

ESTABLISHING AN SPI PROGRAM

It would be quite easy to get bogged down even before beginning. A group can argue for hours on the question: "Are children able to prescribe for themselves starting from about mid-first grade on?" Until you've seen it happen, your answer would probably be, "Of course not!" And the next thought you'd have as a teacher saying "Of course not!" is "What would they need me for?" Argue not. Children can be taught to prescribe for themselves and further, when this becomes a school's goal, the teacher's role changes. She becomes a motivator, an assistant to the youngsters and a partner in learning—an exciting role emphasis.

How to begin? Some might advise jumping in with both feet and saying "Okay kids, let's go study whatever you want to study." Contrarily, the best advice would be to start out as you always have and both you and the youngsters depart into the changes required by SPI, using such a system as the Goal Card when you're ready. Starting out as a benevolent, or not so benevolent, yet stern dictator as far as discipline is concerned, for example, and easing into increasingly more freedom for the youngsters as they get accustomed to handling themselves (a democratic environment), seems to be the right method to use here. Meet the youngsters where they are.

Once you have introduced the materials and have established SPI values such as: it's *boring* to cheat; you won't accomplish what you would like to if you cheat; it's *dumb* to use a material that is either too easy or too hard; it's *smart* to be able to work on your own; etc.—then it is important to discuss the rights of others to learn in an atmosphere conducive to learning. For some, quiet is preferable; for others, it isn't. If a quiet area has not already been designated, the class should be consulted for the decision. After all alternatives have been reviewed and the decision made, the students are to understand that they will be held to it. For example the quiet area should not then be violated by noise. The other areas would not be the opposite of quiet, but rather a place where youngsters can sit around a table together and work and talk together.

With this system, some youngsters will flounder or seem to wander around aimlessly for the whole period. One of two ways of handling these youngsters is to sit tight for a couple of weeks or months until they get bored and finally decide to work. This is a very difficult but possibly the wisest thing to do, remembering that you are every so often trying to lead that child into using an appropriate material and are keeping him out of mischief. Or, you could select a material that you think the youngster is able to handle successfully and ask him to sit down and try it—a little more autocratic but in this case perhaps the most appropriate role to assume. Once the doors for free-flowing, honest, yet courteous pupil/teacher interaction have been opened, communication will soon be forthcoming from the child as to whether or not he wants you to prescribe for him. And should it become an issue, it would indicate that you're well on your way to motivating the heretofore unmotivated wanderer.

The question to consider next is how much time should the youngsters be involved in SPI per week? That question can only be answered in terms of the weight placed upon DPI (District Prescribed Instruction) and TPI (Teacher Prescribed Instruction). State law usually has its prescriptions too. Since the ultimate is 100 per cent, one way of determining might be 50 per cent by the end of eighth grade, 80 per cent by the end of twelfth grade and 100 per cent at the conclusion of undergraduate school, or some such goal statements.

The kind of school design that would promote a separate yet integrated classroom/Learning Center facility to aid in the adoption of SPI is illustrated in this book in Chapter 6, "Designing and Equipping the Learning Center."

EXTENDING THE SPI CONCEPT

The idea has appeared before in the history of education that youngsters should be planning their day in school—that each school day should begin with such planning. The concept then was in terms of the group as a whole. If an independent study program is in existence, however, regular planning on a one-to-one basis can also be facilitated so that the teacher and each student can frequently confer to discuss the "where we are," "where we are going," "how we're going to get there" kinds of ideas. This goal-setting process becomes quite a natural one to facilitate learning. Goal setting, a process leading toward achievement, is indeed intrinsic to daily life, and especially to learning in school successfully. That is why this whole business of Learning Centers, goal setting, improved decision making and finding joy in learning really hang together so crucially. This fact cannot be reiterated enough. Our business in school is to assist and guide youngsters to competently assume the responsibility for their own decision making and provide them with the techniques we know are needed for achieving success in life. Let us never forget, however, that all this assistance cannot come about without warm involvement with the children and the resolution of their social-emotional problems.

If we do indeed accept the SPI challenge, then four basic kinds of goal setting would be taking place:

1. An individual creating immediate goals for himself based upon various test data.
2. A group stating their immediate goals.
3. An individual developing long-range goals.
4. A group planning long-range goals.

The teacher's role here is to "butt out," so to speak, whenever possible, in order to allow for an individual's growth. In other words, the teacher's goal is not to be needed by an individual or group in any kind of crippling type dependency relationship.

A tool to assist the individual student in developing immediate goals could be something like the Goal Card mentioned earlier. Another tool of use to the individual student in developing his long-range goals could be the report card. (See Figure 4-1 for an example.) Methods for promoting group goal setting are encouraging peer group teaching and teamwork and daily or every-other-day lesson planning.

IPI AND THE LEARNING CENTER

Individually Prescribed Instruction (IPI) was initiated at the Learning Research and Development Center at the University of Pittsburgh. Each child's program combines planning, designing and directing to meet his special needs as a learner. IPI requires a Learning Center to function well. A Learning Center does not need IPI to accomplish its goals, however.

In the IPI program of elementary reading and mathematics, various modes of learning are taken into consideration. Individual differences regarding the rate of learning, the extent of preparation and even the various media are taken into account so as to tailor an individual student's learning program to his own particular needs. These needs are determined by taking pre-tests and post-tests as he progresses along the IPI continuum. This continuum consists of sequentially arranged skills according to their degree of complexity. Skill sheets representing various learning styles are available for each skill area.

The rate of speed at which each child progresses along this continuum depends upon his own capabilities. The assignments are given each student by the teacher or teacher's aide. These assignments are called a prescription. A prescription is an individual lesson plan for each student each day.

The student's mastery of the curriculum is judged by curriculum-embedded tests (CET) and post-tests. Before proceeding to the next level, he is required to perform at a competency level of 85 per cent, although this may vary with individual abilities.

The child usually works independently, thus building up his sense of responsibility and confidence in his own knowledge. He begins to realize that learning is a process that is dependent

REPORT CARD

_____ has accomplished the following
goals as indicated by X in the box on the same line.
School Year 19_____-19_____

	Quarters			
ATTITUDES: My goal(s) are:	1	2	3	4
a. To treat my sister nicely at school.				
b. To not have to act like a big-shot so much.				
c.				
EFFORT: My goals are:				
a. To push harder to spell better (to practice my word lists one hour/week).				
b. To work well four hours/week independently.				
c.				
READING: My goals are:				
a. To finish the Hardy Boys series this year.				
b. To achieve through SRA IIa green by Jan.				
c. To renew my library card.				
d. To help Charley learn 100 words he doesn't know by March.				
e.				
MATH: My goals are:				
a. To multiply by two-digit numbers by Jan.				
b. To write my numbers neatly and orderly.				
c. To teach myself how to add fractions using the CTB books.				
OTHER: My goals are:				
a. To talk up more in Social Studies—once a day.				
b.				
c.				
NUMBER OF TIMES ABSENT:				
NUMBER OF TIMES TARDY:				

FIGURE 4-1

INTEREST STUDY PROJECTS:
   1.
   2.
   3.

STUDENT COMMENTS:

TEACHER COMMENTS:

My teacher_____and I have talked about these goals. They
are mine and I intend to see them accomplished this year.

                              _____
                              Signature of Student

_____and I have talked these goals over. They are
ambitious yet achievable. Your support of_____
efforts will be most worthwhile.

                              _____
                              Signature of Teacher

We, _____ parents, are proud of our
youngster's efforts this quarter.

                              1. _____
                              2. _____
                              3. _____
                              4. _____
                              Parent's Signature

Parents' Comments:

Has your youngster improved in his or her:

         Reading and interest to read?

         Showing new learning interests at home?

         Other:

FIGURE 4-1, Continued

on his own participation and initiative. Sometimes he works in the Learning Center.

Helpful in understanding the mechanics of the Learning Center as it interacts with IPI is to describe briefly a typical IPI day, following the progress of a child in either reading or math.

The child gets his own IPI folder from his classroom teacher. This folder is evaluated on a daily basis by the teacher before school begins. A prescription is assigned based on the previous day's accomplishments. The child then fills his prescription by working with individually tailored work sheets. Filling the prescription may require his going to the Learning Center to use its facilities as opposed to utilizing IPI work sheets. If this route is designated, the decision for it is generally arrived at by the classroom teacher and the Learning Center teacher. Their goal is to augment IPI by bringing appropriate materials to the child that would help him develop the skill with which he is having difficulty.

For example, a child doesn't understand how to add "ly" and "ing" to words. He has completed the assigned IPI work sheets but is still experiencing difficulty in mastering the concept. The teacher directs the child to the Learning Center for supplementary material such as the cyclo-teacher, filmstrips, tapes or peer-group tutoring.

The child completes this Learning Center assignment and returns to the classroom teacher to show his progress. The teacher will make another prescription based on the child's Learning Center experience. The result might therefore include further work or a curriculum-embedded test (CET) to check mastery.

Another child's prescription may send him directly to the Learning Center for reference material, discs, filmstrips or manipulative devices. This is an initial prescription and not supplementary.

In IPI, there are as many ways of using the Learning Center as there are individual children. Nonetheless, there are also many IPI classroom activities, too; such as, teacher-directed, small-group instruction, peer-group tutoring or a (total) class seminar directed by the classroom teacher. However, these activities, through team teaching, often become another way of having the Learning Center and IPI interact profitably. The Learning Center teacher may also become involved in reinforcing a skill that the entire group is finding difficult, such as using the card catalog, the index, cross referencing, fractions, measurement, etc. Thus, the Learning Center augments IPI as well as shares much of the same philosophy in educating children.

INTEGRATING IPI AND THE LEARNING CENTER, PHYSICALLY SPEAKING

In a physical sense, the Learning Center is where all IPI materials are housed. Any material that is needed on the pre-tests, work sheets, CET's or post-tests is available in the Learning Center.

There are specific reasons why the IPI materials are located in the Learning Center rather than in the classroom. Grade-level materials cannot be assigned because each child is working on materials based on his level of competency, thus causing an overlapping of grade levels. Conceivably, a third grader may be working on the same materials as a fourth grader and, conversely, this same fourth grader may be trying to master the same skill as the third grader. Obviously the cost of providing a broad range of materials in each classroom is prohibitive and impractical. Ideally, therefore, the centrally located Learning Center provides easy access for all youngsters to IPI work sheets and Learning Center materials. (To achieve such centralization of materials, requires that the staff give up what they heretofore kept in their classrooms. This may sound easy to accomplish but in reality could be a big stumbling block. About the only way this "sharing" can be accomplished is as a natural result of the teacher's involvement in goal setting for the Learning Center. Otherwise, it would take an administrative edict, thus causing resentment and at best half-hearted involvement. Or, it would take reassigning uncooperative tenure teachers elsewhere. Ideally, the first method is best.)

Some of the specific materials that are used as Learning Center activities and in turn are necessary for IPI work are: texts, reading programs (SRA, *Reader's Digest, Literature Sampler*, etc.), books, encyclopedias, dictionaries, tapes, discs, newspapers, magazines and almanacs.

The philosophy and goals of the IPI program and Learning Center are quite compatible. In the multi-media approach of IPI and Learning Centers, both are striving to guide and make available different ways of learning. We know that not all children learn at the same rate or equally as well with the same media and materials. The Learning Center tries to give them the chance to explore many different ways of learning their chosen subjects, just as IPI shows the child different media to use to master a skill.

IPI strives to foster independence, responsibility for one's own learning, confidence in one's knowledge and the realization that learning depends on one's initiative. Many children in IPI write their own prescriptions. This is most significant, in that the child realizes himself what he must do to master a skill and become proficient with it. In other words, the child is diagnosing and is being trained to prescribe for his own learning needs though the original intent was to have the teacher do the prescribing.

The Learning Center strives through the use of Goal Cards and interest study projects to involve children in learning the skills necessary to identify learning goals and how to meet them, whether through prescriptive process for skill development or cross-referencing skill development for interest study.

The Learning Center is concerned with each individual child and assisting him to do his own "thing." In the case of interest study, an evaluation occurs at the completion of a project between the child and his teacher. It is a time when the child analyzes his work and decides what he has learned, judges how he may choose to share what he has learned and then determines his next learning goal.

In IPI a youngster follows a similar process but is evaluating his learning process more frequently, even daily. He finds out what he doesn't know, what he has to learn and is continually guided on how to learn whatever specific skill he is lacking.

These tasks are impossible unless there is communication and cooperation between the classroom teacher and the Learning Center teacher. Conferring on an individual child's needs between teacher, Learning Center teacher and child can thereby bring the desired result of individualizing a child's education.

In this way, IPI is evaluating and bringing growth to the Learning Center and vice versa. Both programs enhance the other. They both focus on individualizing instruction.

These two programs capitalize on providing a youngster with success, as well as providing meaningful experiences for the child by means of their own definition—a key ingredient to making learning desirable, in fact, downright fun.

5

Selection and Duties
of Center Staff Members

How the Learning Center is to be staffed is
dependent upon two main factors: (1) the
degree of commitment to the concept, and (2)
the amount of funding available. A *minimal
staffing* will be considered first, then an *average*
staff and finally the *ideal* one. Basically, minimal
staffing means no Learning Center teacher, the
average staff having one and the ideal staff three,
in addition to a qualified librarian.

Though the term "minimal" is being used
to describe a staffing situation, it should by no
means convey the idea of minimal program
quality as a result. In fact, the minimal staffing
situation requires, and for that matter depends
upon, a whole school's teaching staff being
directly involved in the implementation of a
Learning Center's program. This factor means, in
other words, that more guidance, more trained
human resources are being focused upon each
youngster and the attainment of Center goals
than in the average staffing situation. The
assumption prevails, therefore, that the minimal
staffing can be better than the average which,

due to the presence of a Learning Center teacher, frequently lacks a recognition for the need of total staff involvement.

MINIMAL STAFFING

To operate an elementary school Learning Center, the main leader would be the building principal. If the most desirable circumstance was to prevail, the principal would be one who has had the experience of initiating, organizing and operating a Learning Center. Since there are few thus qualified, it would be advantageous, therefore, to have a principal trained for Learning Centers in such a workshop as the one conducted in Elk Grove Village during the summer school session of 1968. In any event, the principal who desires to initiate a Learning Center must be one who is personally committed to the goals that gives its program meaning. He must be highly organized and above all *not* threatened by staff involvement and decision making. This final criterion is not meant to imply that the principal be the type who is staff dominated to the point where he can make few if any decisions affecting the school's operation and direction without fearing staff revolution. Rather the principal must possess that quality of leadership capable of inspiring creative staff contributions and positive staff involvement.

The principal, in his role as Learning Center leader, will have the job of seeking funds for materials from District and Title II resources. He will survey his school building to find an area that will lend itself to housing materials and provide work areas for the youngsters. The state of the school's library must be taken into account. The help of consultants would be desirable. People such as media experts, architects, Learning Center experts, librarians, etc., would provide valuable insights.

If funds are not available for such an aggressive approach, a more modest inception would be appropriate. In all probability, the key ingredients in a modest circumstance would be creative scheduling, the utmost in staff commitment and cooperation and some minimum funding of about $3,000 for materials. (See Chapter 6 for a suggested materials list containing all pertinent data for ordering.) It must be noted at this juncture that there is the assumption that a library exists and that the $3,000 provides for an embellished resource facility. If library and resource books are not in a building, a minimum initiation budget would be about $10,000.

It would also be the responsibility of the principal, as Learning Center leader, to meet with the staff and discuss the concept and what he has learned regarding its feasibility and the degree of district support for Learning Centers. The goals must be discussed with the staff. A decision should be reached regarding the goals to which they most closely identify. At another time, problems of implementation will be brought up. Moreover, the understanding must prevail that the problems and snags can be worked out. How well they are dealt with, however, is obviously dependent upon the creative, combined energies of the staff, and later of the school's youngsters.

Necessary, in terms of minimum and ideal staffing of a Center, is for each teacher to identify with some project of implementation and/or maintenance of her school's Learning Center program. Ordering materials; cataloging and organizing books and materials for easy accessibility; teaching other staff members how the materials work; training parent volunteers and Learning Center aides; scheduling; developing a school library science curriculum to teach as much about it as early as possible; etc.—all are some key tasks. Most important, however, is the involvement of each teacher with the youngsters from her classes in the Learning Center.

The task of cataloging and organizing books and materials is an enormous one. How well it is done, how carefully library standards are met, will relate in large measure to the success of an ongoing, worthwhile Learning Center program. Therefore, under minimal staffing requirements of a Learning Center, at least one if not two Learning Center aides are required.

QUALIFICATIONS OF A LEARNING CENTER AIDE

The Learning Center aide is a district employee. The aide

should be selected in accordance with the following criteria: pleasantness of appearance; a woman who may or may not be a parent, but if so, a parent of youngsters in a school *other* than the one in which she is to be employed; possess a warmth and genuineness of spirit; have good typing skills; have good command of a foreign language, if necessary; and, above all, be a person who cherishes the idea of efficient organization.

The key task of the aides would be to catalog the books and materials. It is at this point that a trained librarian, in the role of consultant, would help in developing a system of cataloging. She would educate the teachers who have volunteered to be responsible for this phase of Center operation to the system. The aides would be involved in such planning also.

A means of cataloging devised for the Ridge Learning Center in Elk Grove was a simplified version of the Dewey Decimal System. Though it is doubtful that this system at Ridge is original, nonetheless it amounts to this: if a filmstrip, for example, should be numbered 617.36, it was modified to 617. (At the elementary school level, the decimal concept is difficult for a majority of the youngsters to comprehend.) Also, fractionalization seems more sophisticated than necessary at that level. Furthermore, in the process of cataloging materials other than books, cards with a color tipping at the top are used to identify the nature of various media. Blue-tipped catalog cards for filmstrips, brown-tipped for pictures, picture portfolios and vertical file materials, green-tipped for records, orange-tipped for self-operative materials and perhaps red for tape recordings. The major headings on these cards, the color-coded ones, would be subject oriented. They should be organized to give primary consideration to the subject interests of youngsters; such as, dinosaurs, planets, cooking, dolls, etc. Book cards in the catalog, of course, are not color coded. When the materials are in proximity to the books, only one card catalog unit is needed for integrating these cards. (See Figures 3-5 through 3-8 in Chapter 3 for samples of the color-coding system described above.)

The foregoing paragraph indicates a system of cataloging. It has been included here to illustrate the fact that the author cannot help but believe the services of a trained, media-oriented librarian could immeasurably improve upon this system. She could also aid in the organization of the library and its materials as well as give guidance to staff members. This procedure would lead toward a more secure direction of helping all involved to perform their jobs meaningfully and well.

Having been trained in media maintenance, cataloging and general library procedure, the aides would now be ready to work with parent volunteers. At this time, a teaching staff member would perform her responsibility of working in conjunction with the building principal by initiating and organizing the parent volunteer program. A general letter to the parents soliciting their aid; an announcement during a PTA meeting; a gathering to discuss what tasks would be involved; scheduling the times they could help; delegating a home-bound parent volunteer to the job of seeing to it that if one lady can't come a sub will be there; etc.—would all be ways this staff member would go about setting up the program.

THE PARENT VOLUNTEER

The parent volunteer is of great assistance in the Learning Center. The time-consuming tasks of carding books; checking books out; reading (checking and placing in order) the stacks and card catalog file; returning books to the shelves; placing the materials in order; repairing books and materials; typing; etc. can all be capably handled by well-trained, interested volunteers. Unfortunately, it is often the case that people, educated in library science, occupy their time at these tasks when their talents could well be used more creatively.

Parents do a wonderful job. After a while, the more faithful return either a morning or an afternoon or more each week and exercise their initiative by attending to the aforementioned tasks which are ever constant. If left on the shoulder of one full-time individual, these tasks would just about occupy that individual's total time, allowing him but stolen moments for the enormous job of processing books and materials properly. Initiating, maintaining and operating a Learning

Center is no small undertaking. Parents become, therefore, a source of tremendous assistance.

Volunteer parents should be trained carefully and given a clear understanding of the raison d'être of a Learning Center. It helps make their tasks more meaningful and their dedication more intense, provided, of course, that they see the goals of a Center as being significant. Volunteers, educated well, become top-notch emissaries for communicating what the Learning Center is all about. Remember, with them travels evaluations as to whether or not the goals of the program are indeed being met. However, we have yet to meet a parent who does not feel that every penny spent on their Learning Center is money well spent.

Parent volunteers who attend to the types of tasks mentioned earlier are but one kind of human resource. In addition, much could be done to tap the vocational and avocational talents of parents in the Learning Center, and, for that matter, in the classroom as well. For example, a father who may be a stamp collector might be willing to take a few hours away from work to come and hold a discussion group with youngsters similarly interested. A mother who is an accomplished knitter might wish to help a group of youngsters produce satisfying knitted items. A carpenter may have some spare time in the winter to show those interested how to make simple or even complex objects. A mother with ability in arts and crafts could lead youngsters in making objects worthwhile to themselves and related to their interest studies in the Learning Center. The list could easily go on and on. The point is that parents can be a very valuable asset in guiding youngsters toward enjoying learning and developing their ability to see the variety of purposes for learning—purposes that are indeed meaningful to the youngsters as individuals, as people—not just as some strange species labeled "children."

AVERAGE STAFFING

The average staffing situation is of the type found in Elk Grove and other communities. This sort of staffing, which depends mainly on the Learning Center teacher, may seem preferable when the reasoning behind it is that the classroom teacher need not divide her time still further by being a part of the Learning Center program. This reasoning, on the surface, may seem to have merit. As we shall see, however, the quality of a Learning Center in an average staffing setup is dependent upon the talents of two people—the Learning Center teacher primarily, and the building's principal. The quality, therefore, must be considerably limited. Even if a school should be so lucky as to hire a Learning Center teacher who is a creative leader with keen organizational talent, she is for at least a year an outsider to the staff. This negative predicament of a Learning Center teacher is practically unavoidable, because she is doing something "different." It takes quite some time before anyone has even a minimal concept of what she is doing. Generally, from outward appearance, especially if she is an organized individual, it looks as if she has practically nothing to do. Plus, as in Elk Grove, unfortunately, the Learning Center teacher is included in the pupil-teacher ratio, which means each teacher has to have more students in her classroom. Thus, hostility can easily be created rather than cooperation. An interesting fact to note here is that many teachers have turned down the offer of being a Learning Center teacher as well as its salary bonus of $500. Many Learning Centers have been destroyed by giving the teacher extra pay.

Upon becoming this specialized kind of teacher, key advice is usually, "perform services for the teachers—be even so humble as to run their dittos for them." Why the need of such advice? Unless the teachers look kindly upon the Learning Center teacher in this situation, they may not send their youngsters to the Learning Center nor use the facilities that it provides. Moreover, there exists no definite expectation that they do so. The Learning Center teacher who has the primary responsibility for operating the Center is thus relegated to the position of being a currier for favor. And though a sympathetic, knowledgeable principal is of some help, he often lacks the awareness necessary to care enough for a total staff commitment and what it implies. He has not been, after all, a Learning

Center teacher. Furthermore, he generally has his own goals for the school and frequently just doesn't seem to stop and realize that Learning Center goals are sound overall goals of education, worthy of priority positioning in relation to his list. Or perhaps, what has happened results from a tardy specific list of Learning Center goals—therefore this unfortunate dichotomy.

THE PRINCIPAL'S ROLE IN A TROUBLED SCHOOL

The following are some steps the principal of a school which has a Learning Center in trouble needs to do:

- Establish with the superintendent of his district "reasonable" expectations for teacher involvement in their school's Learning Center operation.
- Relate and discuss problems with the Learning Center teacher frequently. She ought to be deeply involved in your goals, too.
- During an in-service workshop discuss the expectations with the staff, indicating that they are a *starting* place and may be added to or revised later on.
- During that same workshop, discuss the Learning Center goals.
- Train staff in Learning Center operation or whatever other activities regarding your school's Learning Center seem appropriate. Maybe if your group is pretty far along they may want to spend some time designing and making some Learning Center materials.
- Call on the superintendent for help with uncooperative personnel, if the situation persists.

THE ROLE OF THE LEARNING CENTER TEACHER

The Learning Center teacher, in the average staffing situation, is hired by the building principal. She meets with him to find out how he views the functions of the Center and how he desires her to relate to him in the performance of her duties.

He lets her know the degree of decision-making power she is to have and what sort of matters he desires to be consulted about. In fact, from the very beginning, the Learning Center teacher should be communicating with all staff members regarding the Learning Center. It would be advisable that some of the time during the teachers' preparation week, before school commences, be devoted to increasing a general understanding as to the Learning Center goals and the role of the Learning Center teacher. This time should be prepared for by the building principal and the Learning Center teacher. The Learning Center teacher, however, would be the one to assume leadership in working with the teachers in this preschool workshop. To think, however, that the workshop would be an end to the need for communication would be a drastic mistake. Communication must indeed be ongoing. In addition, it must be a district expectation of its staff that the Learning Center is also their concern. Too often it has been thought that since we are often "meetinged to death," that only when there is a need should there be a staff meeting—a staff-initiated type situation. This is a good idea if and when a staff has arrived at a high degree of actualization. The staff cannot always know, however, when *they* are needed. To have vital staff involvement there must be collective cause. Close identification with the building's goals, including Learning Center goals and teacher goals, is a key means to the establishment of such cause. Unification of effort can be immensely more effective than having a meeting "if and when we feel like it." An interesting, though perhaps faulty, assumption could be that from the promotion of such a negative attitude toward staff meetings among a staff, what results is negative, nihilistic leadership.

In addition to her role of communications leader, the Learning Center teacher has quite a variety of responsibilities. Following is a list of her various duties:

* Organizes materials and audio-visual equipment for easy accessibility and usability by youngsters and teachers for Center and classroom use.

* Purchases media to promote both Learning Center and school goals.

* Instructs students and staff in how to use all media.

* Directs a school's instructional program in library science.

* Guides youngsters toward the attainment of their learning goals.

* Shares in the responsibility for the total school's program.

* Assists teachers in evaluating achievement of youngsters and in diagnosing learning differences.

* Aids in planning the use of instructional materials in order to promote specific educational objectives in each learning activity.

* Assumes the bulk of responsibility for the preparation of future Center teachers within the district and on an optional basis outside the district.

* May serve as a consultant to educators interested in adopting similar Learning Center programs in their schools.

* Selects, supervises and trains clerical personnel to serve as aides in Learning Center-library areas.

* Aids in interpreting school's goals to the community.

* Supervises the inventorying of all media, including library books and Title II acquisitions.

* Makes recommendations regarding future needs to be met for continued productive operation.

* Is responsible for efficient system of processing all media, including books.

* Investigates, innovates and/or implements new programs to meet past or newly formed Center or school goals.

* Participates in devising a workable, flexible school schedule.

* Interprets school's program to visitors.

* Works with faculty in examining present beliefs and teaching techniques.

* Initiates and supervises volunteer program where needed.

* Participates in district activities to promote Learning Center growth.
* Participates in some form of self-assessment or group dynamics program.
* Seeks growth in the fields of guidance and library science.

The Learning Center teacher is indeed a busy person, who more than earns her salary bonus. Furthermore, because of such a comprehensive role, the Learning Center teacher does need help. More aides can be of help. However, they are of but partial service. To whom besides the building principal, therefore, can she turn for creative planning and problem solving? To whom can she turn for such resourcefulness outside of herself? It seems natural to turn to the school's staff. What, however, can justify this added faculty responsibility?

* The more the staff knows about the Center the more they use it.
* More creative use of the Center—"several heads are better than one."
* Administration's help to re-evaluate curricular and value priorities. Consequently, the redistribution of efforts expected of the teacher (this step is of vital importance).
* More trained personnel to guide the youngsters—as was mentioned earlier—because the teachers are in the Learning Center working with their students.
* Augmented understandings between staff and Learning Center teacher.
* A smoother total school operation.
* A higher esprit de corps.

When such outcomes as these can be envisioned, it seems almost intolerable to proceed under the illusion that the Learning Center teacher can withstand an isolated position— that practically alone she must make the greatest use of the wealth of materials at her command for the good of the school's youngsters; that alone she must reach the faculty to create mutual appreciation for the frustrations each other's jobs impose; that alone she must shoulder the responsibility of misunderstood mistakes she is bound to make in trying to do her job well; that alone she must try to establish communication.

Surfacing here is an obviously strong disposition toward staff involvement. Strong because it is a key to the realization of the more than worthy Center's goals. When creative leadership and a sense of integrity derived from high yet attainable expectations exist, it can inspire creative staff involvement. In unity there is indeed strength. The Learning Center and its director must not be entities. For an effective Learning Center program, a unified though not always agreeing staff, can be an effective corporate team. Whether such cooperation is to exist, however, will of course be dependent upon the district's expectation of their teachers as well as the quality of leadership a principal provides.

QUALIFICATIONS OF A LEARNING CENTER TEACHER

To do the kinds of tasks required of her, the qualifications of a Learning Center teacher would be: leadership ability; vitality; a warmth and sensitivity to youngsters; a minimum of two years teaching experience, preferably in a primary and an intermediate grade; a definite appreciation for the importance of instructing in library science; a guidance orientation; an educationally creative talent; keen organizational ability.

THE ROLE OF THE AIDES

In the average staffing situation, the role of the aides would be similar to that of the aides in the minimal staffing situation and that of the ideal. Below is a list of their responsibilities:

* Supervise youngsters.
* Answer questions of youngsters regarding the materials and their operation—or questions of general procedure; i.e., replies that are not of an instructional, teaching nature.
* Assist students when they so request in checking their tests.

* Are responsible for all A-V equipment—its operation and maintenance.
* Assume filing duties.
* Type such items as letters, requisitions, dittos, stencils, bulletins, memos, work sheets, schedules, etc.
* Care for materials and inventory them.
* Provide supplies for Interest Study Projects.
* Make phone calls regarding many Learning Center matters.
* Operate ditto machines, copiers and mimeograph equipment.
* Make work sheets and teaching aids as needed.
* Help youngsters with their bulletin board contributions and displays.
* Supervise, organize and distribute audio-visual equipment, filmstrips, records, tapes, books, etc., according to established procedure.
* Develop student initiative.
* Keep Learning Center in order.

This list should not be considered complete nor unalterable. Flexibility should be the key. A school's overall individuality will certainly indicate additions and/or deletions from that list. Furthermore, the aides will perform these responsibilities in varying degrees, depending on the immediate needs of the Center or the Learning Center teacher at any given moment. Too, the aides' own competencies will be a significant factor here. Many are the aides, nonetheless, who have met the challenges of their job well. They come to see that their contribution, though frequently an underpaid one, is quite attributive to the youngsters finding the Learning Center program of significance to themselves.

THE PARENT VOLUNTEER

In the average staffing situation, the parent volunteer can also provide a valuable contribution. In this case, however, it would be the Learning Center teacher who would do the initiating and organizing of the program. The building principal would be sought for approval regarding such a program, how it's to be initiated and how implemented.

IDEAL STAFFING

The ideal staffing of a Learning Center would include the students, teacher, aides, building principal, parent volunteers, librarian, Learning Center teacher, arts-and-crafts teacher, performing arts teacher, and four Learning Center aides. Two of the aides and the teachers with their classes would be there to assist youngsters in developing and fulfilling their learning goals. In addition, the two specialty teachers would be of great importance. Too long we have ignored the fact that elementary school youngsters are much more graphically and performance oriented to learning than reading oriented. For many youngsters at that age what is written is still read word by word, fumblingly, and with difficulty in comprehension. These specialty teachers, therefore, would provide each youngster with the opportunity to conclude an interest study or self-teaching project with an activity that would provide him joy and a visible result for his efforts.

Achievement is generally determined by a youngster's degree of reading ability. Since reading disability results from a physical problem, or immaturity (which is in a sense physical), or for psychological resasons, why penalize a youngster by denying him recognition? Rather let the Learning Center provide the resources whereby a youngster can seek his talents, develop them, succeed with them and consequently achieve positive recognition—a very necessary ingredient to healthy growth.

Though the following statement may sound trite, we must forever remember: if a youngster could, he would. He would rather read well, than fairly well. He'd prefer to be a whiz rather than a fizzle in math, etc. Consequently, it is up to us to find out why a youngster is not achieving and what we can do to help him overcome his handicaps. But what about in the meantime? Therein lies part of the beauty of the Learning Center dimension. Success is his. It is really within his grasp. The materials and experiences are there from which he can learn. Guidance is provided to help him proceed, and the opportunity exists to use his talents. How much success he needs or wants is his for the taking. It is there for each youngster as an individual, an individual with one or several areas for potential success. And each area is to be indeed honored both by the individual himself as well as by others.

STUDENT TEACHERS

Assigning student teachers to a Learning Center should be just as logical as assigning them to a grade level or team. Or, better yet, the student teacher should have both experiences. Also, it would be helpful as a prerequisite to demonstrate new materials and to involve student teachers in materials operation, as well as indicate the basic strengths of each of the materials.

As a minimum, each practice teacher needs to be exposed to the philosophy of Learning Centers and the materials that add to the Learning Center dimension. This provides a valuable knowledge whether or not there is a Learning Center yet established in the school to which a practice teacher will eventually apply. By the way, schools with Learning Centers would be contributing quite valuably to a practice teacher by involving her in the program.

DIFFERENTIATED STAFFING—A DIFFERENT SLANT

Another method of staffing the Learning Center and the school is through the use of many auxiliary personnel, such as aides and volunteer community workers. The object, as is generally stated, is to keep the pupil/adult ratio close. As has also been developed elsewhere, differentiated staffing calls for different teacher role definition. It is with this latter point that some thoughts come to mind. If independent study is to play a major role in terms of how a youngster spends his time at school, and if there is a major Learning Center facility developed within a school, then through the differentiated staffing concept, it would be financially feasible to provide increased opportunity to interact and be heard by an adult within the school setting. Here's how: Think of the Learning Center teacher as the guide for about 75-125 students working independently—an independent study specialist. Then think of the regular teachers as group work specialists; such as, discussion motivators, one-to-one "interactionists" and auxiliary personnel supervisors. The domain of the former would be massive, carpeted and well-equipped. The domain of the latter would be cozy rooms for discussion or lab-type rooms serving science, audio-visual, arts-and-crafts needs, project (interest study and assigned) type work, etc. Team teaching, therefore, would be used to increase the pupil/adult (not teacher) ratio, by placing the teacher in a supervisory capacity over clerks and aides. This form of team teaching would require fewer teachers in a building. Thus, the teacher, in addition to being guidance oriented, also becomes a personnel manager, which fits in with independent study programs—a point brought out in Chapter 8.

6

Designing and Equipping
the Learning Center

There are three ways to create a Learning Center facility:

1. Find a centralized location within an existing facility and remodel it.
2. Attach an addition to the school.
3. Build a school with the Learning Centers incorporated.

Before any of these avenues can be taken, however, the staff that is to be involved, teachers, administrators and youngsters, are to determine the goals for its establishment. Then, and only then, would the district be ready to employ an architect to remodel an existing area or build a new school. Also, specific questions have to be answered, and it would be wise to include all school personnel, including the secretary and custodians, in answering them. Remember, too, make the Learning Center a children's room, a "fun-looking" as well as an aesthetic place to be.

I.   *FUNCTION*
   A. How will the staff use the new facility?
   B. How will the Learning Center tie in with the existing building?
   C. Possibility of expansion; overall building or Learning Center?
   D. How will it combine with the library?

II. *REQUIREMENTS*
   A. Square footage required?
   B. Small conference rooms? (Visual control, supervision?)
   C. Audio-visual equipment?
   D. Carrels?
   E. Office areas?
   F. To be incorporated into the existing library, or the library to be moved to new Learning Center site?
   G. A quiet working area?

III. *EXISTING CONDITIONS*
   A. *Converting Existing Areas into a Learning Center*—See Figure 6-1, Scheme 1 as designed by Frederick Johnson, Architect, Chicago, for Elk Grove Village, Illinois.

      1. Location (flow of traffic)?
      2. Mechanical treatment (heat, electricity and plumbing)?
      3. Acoustical treatment?
      4. Possible year-round use?
      5. Usually means adding a new addition to the existing building to replace areas absorbed by the new center.

   B. *Adding a New Learning Center Wing or Pod to an Existing Building*—See Figures 6-2 and 6-3, Scheme 2 as designed by Frederick Johnson, Architect, Chicago, for Elk Grove Village, Illinois.

1. Location (flow of traffic)?
2. Can existing heating system take the addition or must it have its own self-contained heating unit?
3. Type of construction?

C. *New Building*—See Figure 6-4, Scheme 3 as designed by Frederick Johnson, Architect, Chicago, for Elk Grove Village, Illinois. Also, see Figures 6-5 and 6-6 as designed by Joyce Glasser.

1. Location now and future expansion?
2. How will teaching stations be incorporated into the Learning Center?
3. Flow of traffic?
4. Quiet working areas?
5. Sound, light and staff visual control?

The foregoing questions and illustrations suggested by Frederick Johnson (2)* are a beginning, leading toward the key steps to be taken when planning for a Learning Center. They should get you pretty well started, however.

MINIMUM LEARNING CENTER STANDARDS

The following is a general list of standards to be carefully considered both by the district and the architect:

1. Carpeting—wall-to-wall—in quiet-study and office areas.
2. Square footage to accommodate 25 per cent maximum student body enrollment (ultimate enrollment) or else space to expand present facilities. Use 35 square feet per student as a guide.
3. Combination of tables for four and six students, along with individual seating at the junior high level

---

* See Bibliography, page 221.

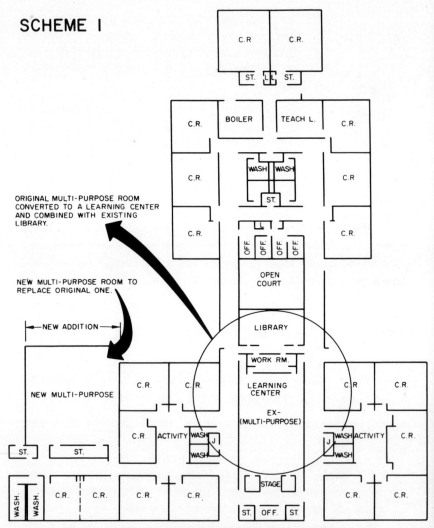

DEVONSHIRE ELEMENTARY SCHOOL FLOOR PLAN

FIGURE 6-1

SCHEME 2

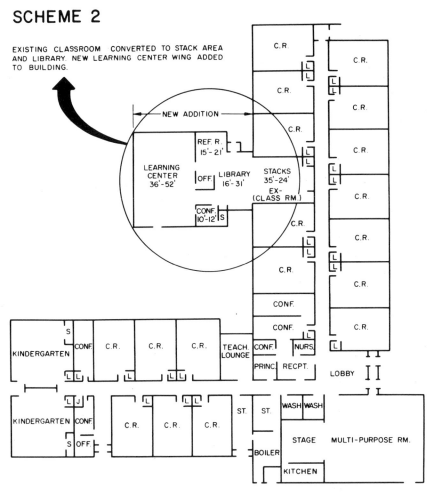

EXISTING CLASSROOM CONVERTED TO STACK AREA
AND LIBRARY. NEW LEARNING CENTER WING ADDED
TO BUILDING.

NEW ADDITION

REF. R.
15'-21'

LEARNING
CENTER
36'-52'

OFF.

LIBRARY
16'-31'

STACKS
35'-24'

EX-
(CLASS RM.)

CONF.
10'-12'

S

C.R.

C.R.

C.R.

C.R.

C.R.

C.R.

C.R.

C.R.

C.R.

C.R.

C.R.

CONF.

CONF.

C.R.

KINDERGARTEN

S

CONF

C.R.

C.R.

C.R.

TEACH.
LOUNGE

CONF.

NURS.

PRINC.

RECPT.

LOBBY

KINDERGARTEN

J

CONF

L

C.R.

C.R.

C.R.

ST.

ST.

WASH

WASH

S

OFF.

BOILER

STAGE

MULTI-PURPOSE RM.

KITCHEN

RIDGE ELEMENTARY SCHOOL FLOOR PLAN

FIGURE 6-2

SCHEME 2

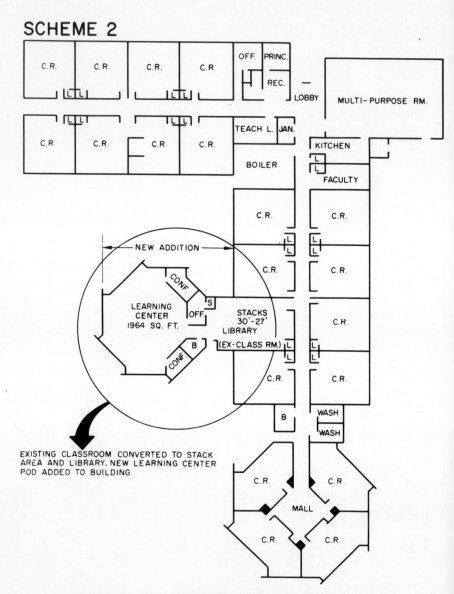

EINSTEIN ELEMENTARY SCHOOL FLOOR PLAN

FIGURE 6-3

SCHEME 3

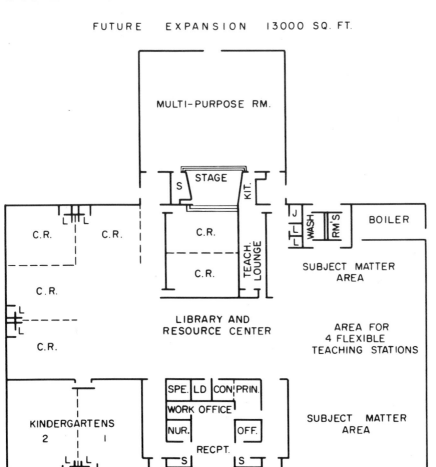

FUTURE   EXPANSION   13000 SQ. FT.

MULTI-PURPOSE RM.

STAGE

S

KIT.

C.R.   C.R.

C.R.

C.R.

C.R.

TEACH. LOUNGE

C.R.

J

WASH.

RM'S

BOILER

SUBJECT MATTER AREA

LIBRARY AND RESOURCE CENTER

AREA FOR 4 FLEXIBLE TEACHING STATIONS

KINDERGARTENS 2

SPE. LD CON PRIN.

WORK OFFICE

NUR.   OFF.

RECPT.

S   S

SUBJECT MATTER AREA

LAKESITE ELEMENTARY SCHOOL FLOOR PLAN

FIGURE 6-4

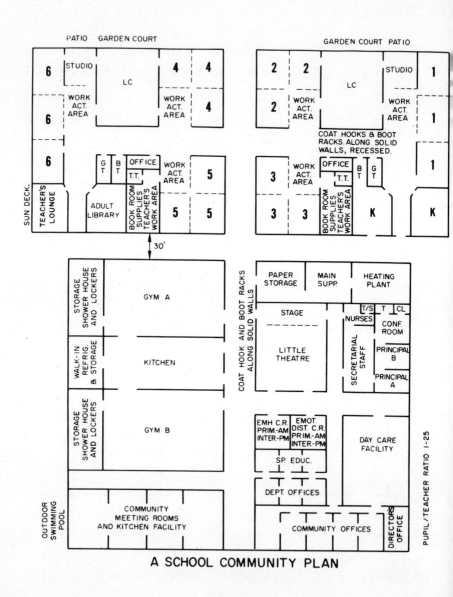

FIGURE 6-5

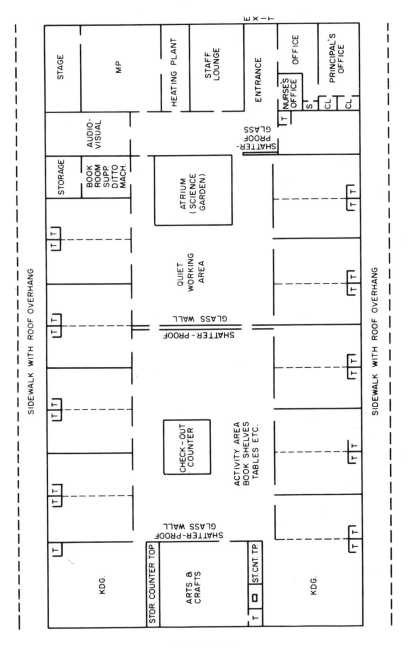

FIGURE 6-6

in modified carrels; comfortable chairs of appropriate height; tables both round and square, with a majority of tables for four; comfortable lounge-type furniture for informal activities.

4. Adequate adjustable, freestanding wood shelving for book collection of 15 books per student, in combinations of counter-height and 6-foot units for junior high and 5-foot units for elementary students; slanted shelving for periodical and picture book display.

5. Special materials storage:

    deep cabinets—Formica counters beneath for programmed materials and learning kits
    dictionary stands
    atlas case
    book drop
    map-print case
    legal-size cabinet for pamphlets
    card catalog
    book trucks
    glass display case—lighted, with lock
    bulletin board

6. Workroom-office area.

    sink
    deep cabinets with Formica counters
    inexpensive steel shelving—plain and divided for periodicals back five years
    2 typewriters
    2 office desks
    1 table
    posture chairs for aides and professionals
    1 legal-size cabinet
    glass partition for supervision

7. Audio-visual equipment.

    2 sound projectors per 600 students
    3 filmstrip-slide projectors per 600 students
    1 opaque projector
    1 record player per five classrooms
    8-10 headsets

a projection screen (60" x 60") per two class-rooms—wall mounted when one to a classroom
1 FM-AM radio per five classrooms
1 television all-channel receiver per five class-rooms
1 video tape recorder (if applicable)
adequate supplies for maintenance and use
adequate storage for ready availability to class-rooms
2 8-mm film projectors
2 cassette tape recorders per 600 students
8 heavy-duty individual filmstrip viewers

8. A-V storage room and production area in an acousti-cally separated room.

Formica counter and cabinets
divided shelving for tape and disc storage
filmstrip cabinet
space for above equipment storage and preview

9. Conference room—with glass partition for super-vision.

a table for six
a table for four
bulletin board
blackboard

10. Materials (for opening day of school).

3,000 books minimum, processed for 200-499 students
5,000 books minimum, processed for 500-1,499 students
25 magazine titles, minimum processed for K-5th grades
70 magazine titles, minimum processed for junior high
3-6 newspapers
extensive learning-kit programmed material col-lections plus funds for teacher material selection
extensive collections of pamphlets, pictures, slides, discs, tapes, realia, etc.
funds for teachers' collection
funds projected over a four-year period to bring

all collections up to educational standards of other existing schools in the district—minimum of ten books per student plus extensive additions in other areas

11. Adequate supplies for processing of materials.

12. Funds for special projects—field trips, talent resource tool, etc.

13. Plenty of linear wood shelving for materials display in quiet working area of Learning Center. One line of shelves should be 2 feet from the floor, and above it another line of shelving at 3½ feet from the floor. Display shelving may be placed 5 feet from the floor.

14. Objets d'art of the "masters" and plenty from the youngsters—paintings, sculpture, ceramics, etc.

15. An alcove suitable for a "chick-a-bator," an aquarium, an ant farm, etc.

16. Plenty of 2-inch wide cork lineage tacked on the walls for hanging youngsters' work.

17. Two walk-in, lighted, shelf-lined, lockable storage closets.

18. A book exchange counter with book slide that would double as a supervision station.

The foregoing standards do not include the acquisition of dictionaries or sets of encyclopedias. It would seem, in fact, that few if any encyclopedias need to be purchased if a school anticipates a large media collection. It is more desirable and realistic for students to study from books, pamphlets, magazines, filmstrips, etc. for the research value. Furthermore, elementary students (as well as secondary students, of course) can indeed be taught to establish a bibliography as well as to appreciate original source material when available.

RECOMMENDATIONS FOR INDEPENDENT STUDY
MATERIALS

The most important form of independent study is student initiated, whether it be for interest study or for skill development. Therefore, materials selection must be done with this key fact in mind. From experience, this fact means that the bulk of the Learning Center's expenditure will be for easy-to-handle-and-comprehend interest study materials: books, records, filmstrips, shortstrips (put out by Encyclopedia Britannica), study prints, films, magazines (like *Hot Rod*), etc. Keep in mind that the most pleasureful learning experience, particularly for youngsters, is usually the graphic-sound-oral-tactile approach. It is important to provide opportunities to see and hear and make things. Reading becomes genuinely pleasurable when there is comprehension. For many youngsters reading remains a halting, word-by-word, sounding-out task for quite some time. So, let's be realistic and provide rich fun-learning materials that these and all youngsters will benefit from.

When ordering books, keep these thoughts in mind:

a. What kinds of information excite youngsters?
b. Is the book easy to read?
c. Does it have lots of colorful pictures?

Many interests of youngsters will require purchasing difficult materials, too, so don't worry too much about not challenging the more talented student.

As for skill-building materials, the following is a recommended list of independent study materials for primary and intermediate Learning Centers:

TITLE	COMPANY	QUANTITY Pri.	Inter.	COST
Reading Interpretations I A-B	California Test Bureau	4	4	$ 8.00
Reading Interpretations I C-D	206 Bridge St. New Cumberland		4	4.00
Reading Interpretations I E-F	Pennsylvania 17070		4	4.00
Reading Interpretations I G			3	3.00
Arithmetic Fundamentals Addition A-B			6	6.00

Arithmetic Fundamentals Addition C	6	6	12.0
Arithmetic Fundamentals Addition D	4	6	10.0
Arithmetic Fundamentals Subtraction A-B	6		6.0
Arithmetic Fundamentals Subtraction C	6	6	12.0
Arithmetic Fundamentals Subtraction D	4	6	10.0
Arithmetic Fundamentals Multiplication A-B	4	6	10.0
Arithmetic Fundamentals Multiplication C		6	6.0
Arithmetic Fundamentals Multiplication D		4	4.0
Arithmetic Fundamentals Multiplication E-F		4	4.0
Arithmetic Fundamentals Division A-B		6	6.0
Arithmetic Fundamentals Division C		6	6.0
Arithmetic Fundamentals Division D		4	4.0
Arithmetic Fundamentals Division E-F		4	4.0
English Language Sentence Patterns		4	4.0
			$123.0

Extra answer sheets—50/title x 19				47.5
(These are a must in order to operate the program.)				$170.5
Time Telling	Graflex, Inc.			
order #65000	General Precision Rochester, New York 14603	8	4	$ 9.0
Perimeters order #65016			6	4.5
Trees, Their Use and Structure order #67010		4	4	6.0
Addition of Fractions order #65006			6	4.5
				$ 24.0

omplete Cyclo- Teacher Kit	John A. Batten 700 Chalet Lane Manchester, Missouri 63011	1	1	$ 99.00
Packages E- Answer Wheels Package-free reinforcers		5	5	24.90 $123.90
ullivan Readers 6 of *each* Books 1-14	McGraw-Hill Book Co. Manchester Road	84		$113.40
6 of *each* Books 15-21	Manchester, Missouri 63011		42	56.70 $170.10

As with most of these materials, the youngsters
an use their own notebook paper as an answer sheet.
'or the above books, you will have to make 4" x 12"
onstruction paper slides (markers), one for each
ook plus extras. These slides cover up the answer
olumn.]

ilot Library IIa #3-5400	SRA 259 E. Erie St. Chicago, Ill. 60611	1	1	$119.90
tudent Record Books #3-5474		6	8	7.00
ilot Library IIb #3-5600			1	59.95
tudent Record Books #3-5674			8	4.00
ilot Library IIc			1	59.95
tudent Record Books #3-274			8	4.00
merican Album-Complete Kit #3-9550			1	67.50
eacher's Handbook #3-9562			1	.40
aleidoscope of Skills #3-9926			8	10.00
eacher's Handbook #3-9925			1	.25 $332.95

eading Skill uilders to be ordered y levels)	Barnell Loft Ltd. 111 South Centre Rockville Centre New York

1st level-books A (70 booklets)	6 sets	4 sets	$ 64.5
2nd level-books B (50 booklets)	6 sets	4 sets	47.4
3rd level-books C (50 booklets)	5 sets	5 sets	47.4
4th level-books D (50 booklets)	4 sets	6 sets	47.4
5th level-books E (20 booklets)		5 sets	19.4
6th level-books F (16 booklets)		4 sets	15.5
			$241.7

(Price includes answer keys for each book in the
set—worksheets plus postage and handling.)
These Barnell-Loft books are outstanding.

Map Skills	to nearest			
Project Book I	Scholastic Repre.	6	6	$ 3.0
Teacher's Educa-	or			
tion Book I	Scholastic Repre.	1	1	.5
Map Skills	902 Sylvan Ave			
Project Book 2	Englewood Cliffs,	4	6	2.5
Teacher's Educa-	New Jersey 07632			
tion Book 2		1	1	.5
Map Skills				
Project Book 3			6	1.5
Teacher's Educa-				
tion Book 3			1	.2

(Answer keys are needed for each pupil booklet.
It would be a good idea to write the publisher
as to suggestions on how to lawfully do this.
Each teacher booklet has the answers. This set
is worth the trouble of procuring.)

Self-Teaching Arithmetic			
Book I	6		23.7
Self-Teaching Arithmetic			
Book II	6		23.7
Self-Teaching Arithmetic			
Book III	6	6	47.4
Self-Teaching Arithmetic			
Book IV		6	23.7
Self-Teaching Arithmetic			
Book V		6	23.7
			$150.4

(For approximately 601 workbooks, two cyclo-teachers,
three pilot libraries and teachers' handbooks)

GRAND TOTAL $1,213.0

Other materials to consider are:

READING LABORATORIES Ia through IIIa
SRA: 1-8 Kits plus record books

Each laboratory includes reading material on a range of difficulty levels to accommodate the various degrees of skill likely to occur at the grade level for which the laboratory is designed. The levels are differentiated by color rather than by grade. Each level includes from 12-20 reading selections (power builders) with accompanying activities for developing comprehension, vocabulary and phonetic and structural analysis of words. As soon as a student demonstrates satisfactory mastery at one level, he moves to the next level. Content of the reading selections included in any laboratory is geared to the interest patterns of students at the grade level for which the laboratory is intended.

READING ROUND TABLE
American Book Company: 1-5

This is a series of paperbacks, which range from preprimer pamphlets to sixth-grade booklets. The stories are contemporary, and each is followed by activities on some phase of structural or phonetic analysis, comprehension, sequence, etc.

READING EXERCISES (Gates Peardon)
Columbia University: 2-6

These exercises are designed to build and strengthen reading skills. This illustrated series provides more than 300 short reading exercises for a wide range of abilities and interests. Useful for developmental and remedial use, the exercises give pupils specific and concentrated practice in reading for different purposes and offer teachers ways of coping with individual differences. Available for reading levels of approximately grades 2 through 6, the booklet consists of a series of short exercises, each followed by questions. As the pupil responds, he must utilize a range of reading skills while answering questions on three important types of reading: What is the story about? Can you follow directions? Do you remember details?

BY MYSELF
Ginn: K-3

This is a set of six programmed reading books, beginning at the preprimer level and extending to the third-grade level. It is phonics-oriented and combines the skills of reading and writing words. It has two tests for each booklet, and pupil performance rate is high. It enables the pupil to build word-study and comprehension skills independently and at his own pace.

MADISON MATH SHOE BOXES

Each box contains a "puzzle" which leads a student to discover a mathematics principle. Inexpensive.

NUMBER BASES AND BINARY ARITHMETIC
D.C. Heath: 5-8

This is a program of bases and binary numeration. It is good but quite difficult. (Two or three copies are enough.)

ASMD - PROGRAMMED ARITHMETIC
Addison-Wesley Publishing Company: 3-7. Complete set— one each of four texts

A program covering the four fundamental operations of ADDITION, SUBTRACTION, MULTIPLICATION and DIVISION, which assists the student in correcting a computational weakness. Each program illustrates the "modern" approach to mathematics; that is, the commutative and associative laws are discussed, as are regrouping and inverse operations.

CORONET LEARNING PROGRAMS
Coronet Instructional Films: 4-6 (Heart, Cells, Solar System, How Scientists Work, Forecasting Weather, Classifying Animals)

These are individually bound books, each taking about 15-18 hours to complete. They are popular programmed material in which learning seems to take place.

FINDING OUT CLASSROOM LIBRARY
Ginn: 4-6

This is a series of 40 study units in science, history, mathematics and literature. Each pamphlet stresses comprehension and reasoning, and encourages studying in depth through research and reference work.

INTRODUCTION TO THE WORLD OF THE MICROSCOPE
(Elementary School Life Science Unit)
National Teaching Aids

These are ten inexpensive microviewers with film-strip slides. Information is given in reading form and then strips are used to demonstrate points made in the printed discussion.

Sample inclusion: From Egg to Chick
How a One-Celled Animal Divides
From Flower to Fruit
Harmful and Helpful Bacteria
Cells of Plants and Animals
Egg to Tadpole to Frog
Plants That are Not Green
How Seeds Travel
Life in a Pond
Parts of an Insect

LET'S FIND OUT
Imperial Productions, Inc.: 3-6

This is a set of four tapes on the subjects of the moon, farm, water, planets. This is better classroom material, as it would be an excellent tool for introducing or summarizing a unit. A teacher's guide is included and suggests related activities.

THE GREEN PLANT
Learning Materials, Inc.:

This includes three science research units, each with

problem and background cards, experiment cards, procedure cards and student research books. The experiments are progressively difficult. These units can be worked independently or in small groups.

Wall Charts — Pictorial Charts, Educational Trust, 132 Uxbridge Road, London, W. 13, England. Chock full of information. Fine reference tool. Unusual coverage of certain topics in poster form never seen before.

Book and Record Sets — Columbia Record Sales Dept., 51 West 52nd Street, New York, N.Y. 10019. Fully illustrated books with companion records in which books are read word-for-word. Selections include preschool through intermediate grade levels.

Disc Recordings — Educational Record Sales, 157 Chambers Street, New York, N.Y. 10007. Outlet for extensive collection. Fine description of content. Runs gamut of curriculum areas.

Realia — Alva Museum Replicas, Inc., 3030 Northern Blvd., Long Island City, N.Y. 11101. Fine sculpture reproductions. Especially exciting:

    a. Rosetta Stone Unit.
    b. Pictographic and Cuneiform Unit.

Included in these units are actual stone tablets and student activity sheets, encouraging discovery in the manner of archeologists.

Sound Filmstrips — Warren Schloat Productions, Inc., Pleasantville, New York 10570. Exceptionally fine material on art history, folk songs in history, minority groups and anthropology. Excellent interweaving of art, music, etc., with an historical period. Fine color reproductions.

Games — World Wide Games, Inc., Box 450, Delaware, Ohio 43015. Nice variety.

Film Loops — Ealing Film Loops, 2225 Massachusetts Ave., Cambridge, Mass. 02140. Excellent quality. Loops on Pilgrims, Beginning of U.S. Industry and Settling the East are exceptional.

Transparencies — DCA Educational Products, Inc., 4865 Stenton Ave., Philadelphia, Pa. 19144. Attractive, accurate materials. Has emphasis on science.

Film Loops — Doubleday & Company, Inc., School and Library Division, Garden City, Long Island, New York 11530. Full selection of cartridge films, many in area of social studies of infrequently sound content. Good choice of sound film loops. Excellent catalog.

Filmstrips — Life Filmstrips, Time-Life Building, Rockefeller Center, New York, N.Y. 10020. Superior material. Seventy frames average. Well-reproduced from magazine presentations.

Prints of Original Source Material — Grossman Publishers, 125A East 19th Street, New York, N.Y. 10003. Each "Jackdaw" is a packet of original source material to underscore the full meaning of a specific historic or scientific topic. Each contains broadsheets, facsimile reproductions of original documents, etc. Excellent teacher's guide.

Filmstrips — Yale Pageant of America Filmstrips, U.S. Publishers Assoc., Inc., 386 Park Ave., South, New York, N.Y. 10016. Fine material in area of American History based on accurate reconstructions. Unusual attention to detail. Excellent authorities. Black and white.

Disc Recordings — Bowman Records, Inc., 622 Rodier Drive, Glendale, California 91201. Established jobber. Very broad selection.

Spoken Arts, Inc., 59 Locust Ave., New Rochelle, New York 10801. For Humanities enrichment and supplementary use.

Folkways/Scholastic Records, 906 Sylvan Ave., Englewood Cliffs, New Jersey 07632. Good selection in all curriculum areas. The range is from primary on up.

Caedmon Records, Houghton Mifflin Company, 53 W. 43rd Street, New York, N.Y. 10036. Leader in

field of spoken-word recordings. Emphasis on
literature. Most are also on tape.

Listening Library, 1 Park Ave., Old Greenwich,
Conn. 06870. Wide selection in many subject and
interest areas.

Filmstrips — Sound — Weston Woods, Weston Conn.
06880. Outstanding primary material.

The *New York Times* Book and Education Division,
299 W. 43rd Street, New York, N.Y. 10036.
Superior quality, up-to-date coverage of current
events. Some with sound.

Games — Wff 'n Poof Publishers, Box 71, New Haven,
Conn., 06501. Fine games for development of logic,
reinforcement of math concepts, etc., and still
remain recreational. From first grade through college.

Stancraft Products, 1621 E. Hennepin Ave., Min-
neapolis, Minn. 55414. Good selection of games
and puzzles. A source for Setko puzzles.

Tapes — Wollensak Teaching Tapes, Minicom Division, 3M
Co., St. Paul, Minn. 55101. Tapes are packaged like
K- 8 a book with 30 student work sheets plus a teacher's
manual. Covers several subject areas.

Imperial International Learning, 247 W. Court
K-12 Street, Kankakee, Illinois 60901. Of special interest: "Meet the Authors"; "Science Experiments" and "Intermediate Math Program."

Tapes Unlimited, 13113 Puritan Ave., Detroit,
Michigan 48227.

Pamphlets — Life Educational Reprint Program, Box 834,
Radio City Post Office, New York, N.Y. 10019.

Slides — 3M Company, International Microfilm Press, Box
720, Times Square Station, New York, N.Y. 10036.
Slides of great art from the museums and galleries
of the world. Also, good supplementary materials
for study of ancient and modern history.

Miscellaneous — Social Studies School Service, 4455 Lennox Blvd., Inglewood, California 90304.

Hubbard Scientific Corp., 2855 Shermer Road, Northbrook, Illinois 60062. Superior materials.

WEATHER AND CLIMATE LABORATORY
SRA: 4-6 lab plus record books

Children are given opportunity to learn by observing and inquiring. Planning, predicting and experimenting allow the child to analyze and draw conclusions. This lab needs a great deal of teacher direction.

PROGRAMMED CHESS
BRL: 3

This program takes a student who knows nothing about chess through a complete program. The last part of the program includes moves and plays which the student must complete. It's good to have a chess set for this. Establish careful guidelines for this program's use. It's very good but can be misused.

WHERE TO PURCHASE MATERIALS

Below is a list of materials companies. It would be a good idea to send to them for current catalogs. Check all prices listed earlier for any changes.

Addison-Wesley Publishing Company, Inc. .	3220 Portar Drive Palo Alto, California 94304
Allied Educational Council	5533 South Woodlawn Ave. Chicago, Illinois
Allyn & Bacon	Rockleigh, New Jersey 07647
American Book Company	300 Pike Street Cincinnati, Ohio
Appleton-Century-Crofts	440 Park Avenue, South New York, N.Y. 10016
Barnell-Loft	Rockville Center New York, N.Y.

Beckley Cardy .... 1900 N. Narragansett Avenu
                                    Chicago 39, Illinois
Behavioral Research Laboratories .... 780 Welch Road
                                    Palo Alto, California
Bell & Howell .... 7100 McCormich Road
                                    Chicago, Illinois 60645
Benefic Press .... 1900 N. Narragansett Avenu
                                    Chicago, 39, Illinois
Bureau of Audio-Visual Instruction ...... University of Colorado
                                    University Ext. Division
                                    Boulder, Colorado
California Test Bureau .... 206 Bridge Street
                                    New Cumberland, Pennsylva
                                    17070
Cenco Educational Aids .... 1700 Irving Park Road
                                    Chicago, Illinois 60613
Columbia University Press .... Bureau of Publishers
                                    New York, N.Y.
Coronet Instructional Films .... 65 East S. Water Street
                                    Chicago, Illinois 60601
Cuisenaire Company of America .... 9 Elm Avenue
                                    Mt. Vernon, New York
Elementary Science Study .... Box 415
                                    Watertown, Massachusetts
Encyclopedia Britannica .... 425 N. Michigan Avenue
                                    Chicago, Illinois
E-Z Sort Systems, Ltd. .... 45 Second Street
                                    San Francisco, California 94
Field Enterprises .... Merchandise Mart Plaza
                                    Chicago, Illinois
Follett & Company .... 1010 West Washington Blvd.
                                    Chicago, Illinois
Gates Peardon .... Teacher's College
                                    Columbia University
                                    New York, N.Y.
Ginn & Company .... 450 W. Algonquin Rd.
                                    Arlington Heights, Illinois
Graflex .... Ben Price
                                    1345 W. Diversey Pkwy.
                                    Chicago, Illinois 60614

Harcourt Brace Jovanovich	7555 Caldwell Avenue Chicago, Illinois
Harper & Row	2500 Crawford Avenue Evanston, Illinois
D. C. Heath & Co.	1815 Prairie Avenue Chicago, Illinois
Holt, Rinehart & Winston	645 N. Michigan Avenue Chicago, Illinois
Houghton Mifflin	1900 South Batavia Avenue Geneva, Illinois
Ideal School Supply Co.	8316 S. Birkhoff Chicago, Illinois
Imperial Productions	247 West Court Street Kankakee, Illinois
Keystone View Company	Meadville, Pennsylvania 16335
Learning Materials, Inc.	425 N. Michigan Avenue Chicago, Illinois 60611
Lyons and Carnahan	407 East 25th Street Chicago, Illinois
Macmillan	Brown & Front Streets Riverside, New Jersey
Madison Project	8356 Big Bend Blvd. Webster Grove, Mo. 63119
McGraw-Hill Book Company	330 W. 42nd St. New York, N.Y. 10036
Charles E. Merrill	1300 Alum Creek Drive Columbus, Ohio
National Tape Recording Service	University of Colorado Boulder, Colorado
National Teaching Aids	120 Fulton Avenue Garden City Park, New York 11044
Noble & Noble	67 Irving Place New York, N.Y.
A. J. Nystrom and Company	3333 Elston Avenue Chicago, Illinois
Reader's Digest Service	Howard Rehn 8151 South Knox Street Chicago, Illinois 61652

Scholastic Magazines & Book Services . . . .   904 Sylvan Avenue
                                                 Englewood Cliffs, New Jers

Science Research Associates . . . .   259 Erie
                                                 Chicago, Illinois

Scott, Foresman . . . .   1900 East Lake Avenue
                                                 Glenview, Illinois

Silver Burdette . . . .   460 S. Northwest Hwy.
                                                 Park Ridge, Illinois

Teaching Machines, Inc. (Div. Grolier) . . . .   575 Lexington Avenue
                                                 New York, N.Y. 10022

University of Illinois Press . . . .   University of Illinois
                                                 Urbana, Illinois 61803

IN SUMMARY

As this chapter indicates, there is much to consider when deciding to initiate a Learning Center. The natural question that comes to mind is: Is it worth it? Resoundingly, yes!

7

Setting Up an
Independent Study Program

COMMITTING YOURSELF
TO THE CONCEPTS

Philosophically, the desirability of independent study programs and facilities is quite similar at the elementary, junior and senior high school levels. The theme of teaching youngsters how to be responsible, how to make decisions and how to organize their activities, consistently emerges as the relevant basis for instituting programs for independent study. At the Lakeview High School in Decatur, Illinois, such needs have indeed been felt, as elsewhere, and have precipitated an admirable independent program to be shared here.

Perhaps as a springboard to the work under the leadership of Richard J. Bodine and Gary D. Lonnon, two challenging questions should be presented: Why are you interested in independent study? Do you really believe students are thinking, responsible individuals? Many students, including the gifted, are lost because they do not feel they are being given the opportunity to grow as individuals. If you believe this, perhaps what you are looking for is independent study. Although it will not answer all of education's problems it is perhaps an answer to some.

135

Schools are handed the task of assisting students to learn to be responsible individuals and citizens. They *must* assume this kind of task, especially since the biggest single activity of most young people is going to school. By the time the average American has reached the age of 18, he has spent more than 12,000 hours in school. In comparison, the church would have to have attendance 422 Sunday mornings a year to have equal time.

The reader may say at this point, "This is not particularly new. We have been hearing much of this since *Sputnik* made its well-publicized takeoff better than ten years ago, and schools have made many changes in that time." However, most of these changes were made in the area of increasing the amount of content that students were being given, but changes to develop responsible behavior have not kept pace. This is where independent study provides help. Some years ago, Lakeview High School embarked on an experimental program in independent study. The top 20 freshmen were ranked in relation to I.Q. test scores and achievement test scores. From this 20, matched groups of ten were selected—one for control, one for experiment. The control group was to have classes as usual. (Even the usual at Lakeview is somewhat innovative—but that is another story.) The experimental group was to be released from required attendance in all courses except physical education and foreign language, where attendance was required because of experimental design and accreditation. Although they had the privilege of attending any class offered in the school, regardless of teacher or sequence, they received grades only for those courses for which they enrolled in the fall. They were to receive a grade of either "A" or "B" in those courses. They were required to be at school during schooltime, but they could receive permission to leave to make use of other resources in the community. The student had the responsibility of making his own decisions, such as: Should I go to class? If so, which classes and what days? Which teacher's section should I attend, if I attend? What should I assign myself? How should I evaluate myself—using grades, or is there a better way? Should I study mathematics and English today, spend the next few days completing a study I'm excited about in social studies or maybe do nothing at all? Teachers were to play a new role also. A seven-member interdisciplinary team was assigned, as part of their duties, to work with these students. They were to be advisors working more or less as equals, solving problems together when asked to help by the students.

How did it work out? It didn't go exactly as planned. At first the students didn't believe that any school would give students that much freedom and trust them too. (There were a few teachers who didn't believe it should happen either.) The students gradually tried to see if they were actually given all the freedoms promised. During this early period, productivity of the students dropped off to practically nothing. It was very difficult for teachers to stand by and watch students do nothing, particularly those students who had been getting top grades. However, a sufficient number of teachers held out in their new roles to test the idea and they have been thankful that they did. The "goof-off" period ranged from six weeks to several months, but the teachers now consider this "goofing off" by the students as the most valuable part of the program. This period brought about the desired objective of the program—students taking responsibility for their own learning. Their productivity emerged greater than before. They actually changed from captive students to learners.

During this time, these young people had to find out some things about themselves: Who am I? Where am I going? How am I going to get there? What responsibilities do I have to take upon myself? The student's self-image emerged from the shadows into a much stronger form that gave direction to his learning program. It is interesting to note this carried over into extracurricular activities. From the experimental group came class officers, publication editors, student council members, varsity athletes, and varsity cheerleaders, at twice the rate of occurrence of the control group.

Early in the program, another problem arose that stifled independence on the part of the student. Students were guaranteed an "A" or "B." Highly motivated students wanted to know what they had to do to get an "A," so the responsibility for their study was passed right back to the teacher, defeating the whole idea of students taking responsibility. It was resolved finally by giving students the freedom to fill out their own grade cards. The students learned grades were not too significant as an effective means of evaluation. This brought about another contribution to the learning of students. What is meaningful evaluation? Grades did not tell them why something was satisfactory or not, nor did it tell them how to improve it. Many times it measured whether they had memorized a sufficient number of facts, disregarding whether they were able to use them or not. A few times it even measured how many times they agreed with the teacher and her bias. They tackled the problem of evaluative thinking and have made good progress towards learning how to evaluate their school products plus their other activities. As an example, evaluation may take this form: "Mrs. Baxter, my intention was to study the causes of the Arab-Israeli War and be able to be as objective as possible in reporting my findings. Would you please take a look at my report and see if I have slanted my remarks or passed judgment for or against either side?" This same student may ask another teacher to judge his same report on the basis of factual accuracy or on some other basis. Perhaps he might ask his peer group or someone in the community to pass an opinion on some other criteria. Students soon learned that part of good evaluation was the selection of criteria to give them the needed information and the selection of persons who could and would pass judgment competently.

The experimental students gained some insight into learning as well as did the teachers involved. Learning could take place and be enjoyable at the same time. It could take place outside the classroom. It could be frustrating; there were no definite answers, and sometimes none at all. Learning how to learn, how to solve problems, making decisions from differing data, judging the value and source of the data collected, finding sources of information—these things · were found to be as valuable, if not more so, than what had been happening in some classrooms. Teachers found discussing ideas and concepts with students as equals an enjoyable learning experience. It changed the role of the teacher completely—to one that was more challenging and more rewarding.

Do you feel independent study is an effective way to deal with some of the problems of schools previously mentioned? It is accepted by many educators that independent study deals with all of these problems rather well. Already mentioned has been the students taking responsibility for their own learning, which will not be as apt to stop when formal schooling is completed. This cannot be substantiated as yet, since the first group at Decatur Lakeview will only be seniors at this time. However, two of the original ten are planning to skip their senior year of high school and attend college this year. This will permit feedback a year earlier than expected. The responsibility gained through participation in this program should help them make adjustments in a changing world.

The program will be of particular help to those students who do not seem to be able to work under a highly structured system, especially when it is geared to students of average or below average ability and coupled with a low sense of motivation and responsibility. Paul E. Torrance pointed out in his speech at the convention of the National Association for Gifted Children in May, 1968, creative children needed "time out" from school's curriculum to think. If not given the opportunity to do this, many of them will drop out of school in order to get their "time out" period. Independent study, as described, can provide this opportunity. It allows an "unstructured" person, as well as other students, to learn to make decisions by actually making them. If students make a mistake, it should be in a friendly climate. Improved academic achievement, as such, was not one of the major objectives of the Decatur Lakeview program. It was not considered as important as the other aspects. At the end of the first two years of the program, both student groups were given achievement tests; the experimental group did as well if not better than the control group, but not at a statisically significant level. It can be safely stated that they did equally as well, plus gaining all the learnings that are not measured by achievement tests.

Another aspect of the program at Decatur was the

greater freedom that had been given to all students. During unscheduled time (other than scheduled classes) all students were granted the freedom of selecting quiet study in the resources center, semi-quiet group study in the old study hall or going to the cafeteria which served as a student lounge.

The independent study program at Decatur Lakeview was extended last year to another group of freshmen and was also introduced into the junior high. Additional expansion is slated for the coming year.

Fifth-and sixth-grade students in the Empire School in Freeport, Illinois, have been conducting their program in a similar fashion to Decatur Lakeview for some years now. They expect the children will go through three steps of increasing independence before arriving at complete independent study. Several of them, like their older counterparts in Decatur, choose to follow a similar outline to what their peers use in the classroom. They even attend classes from time to time when the class schedule appears to be useful and interesting. The results have been good. Independent study can be done at younger ages also. One suggested way is to give larger and larger blocks of time each year for independent study. This may start out as time given them after they finish whatever else has been assigned in the room. Gifted students frequently finish sooner than others. It must soon become more than this, if it is to be effective in meeting the goals of independent study. Begin by giving children larger time blocks in which they are not responsible to teachers for assignments or for evaluation during this "free" time.

Are there other schools attempting this type of program? Yes, there are. Most of them are limited programs. For example: An English teacher may offer the gifted students in her senior class English on an independent basis following many of the same ideas as Decatur, but restricting the students to the study of English and to the time period they would usually be in English class. Some of these schools leave out the student self-evaluation, which makes one seriously question how independent it is. Do you think you could institute an independent study program in your school? It is a program that can be set up in many schools. To give a specific answer would depend on certain conditions. If the conditions summarized below could be met, an independent study program in your school is a good possibility:

1. A belief that students are people, individuals and can be trusted.
2. A student can be given the opportunity to make his own assignments as part of, or in place of, his regular school program.
3. The student will be able to make decisions concerning evaluation of his work and progress. This is to be more than just assigning a grade.
4. A school and teachers that will tolerate the "goof-off" period, so the student will have the opportunity to take the responsibility for his own learning.
5. Teachers who will be willing to try this new teacher role.

If the foregoing qualifications are met, you can expect these things to happen to students:

1. They take responsibility for their own learning.
2. They become more self-reliant.
3. A better self-image is developed.
4. Continuous learning can be expected after formal schooling is completed.
5. Responsible leadership will be evidenced.
6. Academic achievement will be as high if not higher than before.
7. Attitudes toward learning will be improved.

REORGANIZING SCHOOLS FOR TODAY

In other words, what can educators do to improve that experience to which children are subjected for a major portion of their early life?

We can first look at the resources available in one's own school community. A careful and realistic appraisal of these resources will show that the major resource is the children. This is true not only in terms of quantity but also quality. With this in mind, coupled with the realization that "kids" are what education is all about, let us examine some possible changes for increasing the quality of education. We agree that children are different and unequal in their abilities, aptitudes, personalities and characteristics. Children do not progress in all school subjects at equal rates. Children entering school at chronological age six may differ as much as four or five years in mental age. Furthermore, as children advance through school, the spread in achievement widens. Education, must, therefore, be a matter of individual student consideration within a structure that recognizes and capitalizes upon the individuality of each and every consumer. The school must allow individual students to pursue their studies at rates commensurate with their individual abilities. It must provide each student with an opportunity to succeed, or at least avoid failure, in reaching these personal achievement levels. The school must grant each student a meaningful share of the responsibility for directing his own educational program. The school must encourage each student to develop an inward desire to learn, as opposed to a desire based only on outside pressures, such as adult approval, grades, tests, credits and promotion. It must provide students with the opportunity to pursue study programs different from or separate from the study program now provided.

Schools which continue to operate with rigid time schedules, dictating when a child may move from one level of learning to another cannot meet these needs. Schools which continually refuse to recognize individuality in actual practice are little better than no school at all. Schools which fail to recognize the differences in the raw material they receive today from the raw material they were given yesterday and continuously produce the same product today as they turned out yesterday, should not survive. We can ill afford to continue to produce the well-educated citizen of 1917.

Children are coming to the schools with more and more knowledge, much of which can be attributed to the impact of television, and must leave the schools and enter a world that is becoming more and more impersonal. They are faced with the likely prospect of increased technology, resulting in a major readjustment of life patterns. Very probably the balance between time spent working and leisure time will shift in favor of leisure. This major adjustment, coupled with the increasing necessity to continue learning in order to survive, will demand skills and attitudes not now being developed.

What then can be done, with the resources available, to create an educational climate to meet the needs of youth today and at the same time build in a flexibility to cope with the changing tomorrow? The initial step should be an overhaul of the existing curriculum. Curriculum committees composed of professionals, students and appropriate community resource people should be formed with the task of constructing a new curriculum. They should assess what is currently being used in terms of content and materials to determine what should remain and what should go. They should examine other content for possible additions. Thus, each committee would collect a large body of content material for each subject area. The committee would then divide this material into small courses. Although no fixed time limit need be set, the courses should be of a length that would allow the majority of students to complete a course in six to nine weeks.

The committee would have to make certain decisions about these unit courses. First, considering state, federal and accrediting agency time requirements, it needs to decide how many units require completion by the student to qualify for graduation. The units should be constructed in such a manner as to be as nonsequential as possible. However, the committee would decide what units should be required of all students. For example, a social science curriculum of 32 units might be offered and 16 units required for graduation. But, the committee might feel that three of the units should be taken by all students. Furthermore, some realistic system of prerequisites might need to be established. These need not, nor should not, be as extensive as the prerequisite system of a college. This should be employed only to account for that sequencing that could not be eliminated. This structure provides for the individual selections of curriculum to meet the needs and interests of the individual. All courses of the curriculum do not have to be offered each year. However, since no restriction would be placed on the course in terms of grade level of the child, this should pose no problem. The smaller the school, the less often a course might be offered.

To adopt this curriculum organization and continue to teach each course much the same as we now teach our courses, would represent no significant change in terms of meeting individual needs. We must, therefore, investigate alternate methodologies for dealing with the content. There are five approaches that appear most appropriate. They are content seminars or small discussion groups, continuous progress, performance criteria, individualized instruction and independent study. These five approaches are often confused or interchanged. Therefore, it will be necessary to carefully define each term and discuss the relative merits of each approach.

CONTENT SEMINARS

Content seminars or small discussion groups represent the most traditional approach of the five being considered. However, there are some basic distinctions between these groups and a normal classroom. The most obvious difference is size. Whereas traditional class size ranges between 20 and 30 children, seminars should include no more than 15 students and ideally should range in size between four and ten students. Whereas the normal classroom is conducted as an autocratic society with the teacher as the leader and dominator of the discussion and the student as the servant and recipient of the "truths" of the teacher, the seminar is a student-centered discussion with all members of the group given an equal opportunity to speak and be heard. The seminar may operate with or without a teacher. It may operate with or without an assigned leader, and the leader could be a student, a teacher, another professional or a community resource person. It may begin with or without a chosen topic for discussion. It may be a regularly scheduled activity or it might be scheduled only when a definite need arises, as requested by either the students or professional staff.

The seminar serves as a laboratory for mastering the skills of handling and developing interpersonal relationships. Participants are given the opportunity to express ideas, test theories, and collect the thoughts of others. Each participant is responsible for developing the skills necessary to communicate his thoughts and feelings to others in the group, as well as receive their thoughts and feelings. The seminar serves to impart new knowledge from several sources to each participant. Its greatest advantage is providing the opportunity for each member to develop the social skills for relating to other people. It serves as a laboratory for trying new behaviors and receiving feedback concerning those behaviors exhibited.

Seminars are not easy to conduct. Role changes expected of the adult members of the group and the students are difficult to develop. Adults are accustomed to dominating discussions involving children and find it difficult to communicate with them when they are placed in the position of having no special distinction other than being the oldest member of the group. The students expect the adult to play the accepted role of director and major discussant and have difficulty adjusting to a change in the stance of the adult. The most critical problem to be solved in developing a successful seminar is the lack of trust within the group—the adults for the students, the students for the adults and the students for the other students. Without ample practice and a built-in feedback process, the seminar will most likely become a small-scale traditional classroom.

CONTINUOUS PROGRESS

In the continuous progress approach, a continuum is developed representing the subject matter sequence to be covered in the course. All students in the particular course begin at a common starting point and progress at their own rate, competing only against their own former achievement. The course is completed after a prescribed amount of time has been devoted to it. Minimum requirements, behaviorally stated, may or may not be established for a course. Continuous progress basically accounts for individual differences that can be attributed to variations in learning rate. In continuous progress, there is no class activity conducted that would resemble a traditional classroom approach. Instead, the teacher works with individual students or small groups of students having a similar problem while other members of the class work individually or in small peer groups.

There are two basic shortcomings of the continuous progress approach. First, the sequence is established and by its nature precludes a student's learning part B of the continuum until part A is mastered. Second, a continuous progress course generally does not make provisions for a student to explore in greater depth any portion of the continuum or branch out to a related field of study at some point along the way. The reason for this is that the basic goal is for the student to complete as much of the continuum as possible according to his individual rate of learning.

PERFORMANCE CRITERIA

The performance criteria approach is similar to continuous progress, in that basically the same type of continuum representing the subject matter sequence is established. However, students will start at varying points on the continuum and strive to attain a prescribed goal (behaviorally stated), the performance of which signifies the completion of the course. Thus, no time limit is established. This approach accounts for individual differences due to rate of learning and readiness level. This approach also allows the student to move back and forth along the continuum as well as explore in depth any point along its course. Since a time limit does not exist, a student may explore related fields at any point. The classroom activities would closely resemble those in continuous progress.

The major problem encountered with the performance criteria approach is the establishment of the goal. Professionals argue that all learning cannot be assessed by a behavioral display. Much of the problem here is the determined reluctance of professionals to accept evidence of success other than tangible products, such as paper-and-pencil tests or written or constructed projects. Furthermore, most persons continue to seek a single behavior sample that will indicate success of the total performance.

If we cannot establish some behavioral goal that will indicate the degree of comprehension, then we probably should not ask students to attempt to learn things which cannot be measured with any real degree of accuracy. However, we will also need to collect different kinds of data to measure performance, rather than rely on a single piece of data or multiple samples of a single kind of data.

THE NATURE OF INDIVIDUALIZING INSTRUCTION

The essential feature of individualized instruction is that one teacher works with one student. The individual student-teacher conference must be a part of any program legitimately entitled "individualized instruction." In this particular approach, no set body of content is prescribed for any course. Instead, the student will select material from the broadly defined subject matter of the course that he wishes to study. The student and the teacher will cooperatively devise a course of study to meet the needs and interests of the student, and they both will decide how to evaluate his performance. The teacher serves as a consultant to the student, assisting him when he expresses a desire for help. This aid may take any or all of the following forms: assistance in procuring materials, assistance in finding resource persons, assistance in the adjustment to this method of study, assistance in interpreting resources and assistance in integrating knowledge from different sources.

A major difficulty in individualized instruction lies in the initial stages of the course. The student is sometimes reluctant, and at other times lacks the knowledge about the subject area, to make a decision about what he wishes to study. When this happens, the teacher is often too eager to impose suggestions on the student that represent the vested interests of the teacher rather than the needs of the child. Also, teachers have a tendency to demand that the student describe fully what he intends to study and how he intends to study at the outset of the course, and then force the student to comply with this early decision.

A large portion of this difficulty might be overcome by providing, as the required units of the curriculum, survey courses in each general field; such as, mathematics, English, humanities, science, social science, leisure activities, etc. This would provide the student with some general background about the subject matter of the course in order to help make the initial decision about what to study. Teachers should take a stance in each course that would allow the student to change directions, when he could present a reasonable argument in terms of his needs and interests for doing so.

This approach to instruction includes provisions for handling individual differences due to interests, needs, learning rates and learning styles.

INDEPENDENT STUDY

The fifth approach, independent study, is the most liberal of the approaches outlined. For independent study, no set body of content is prescribed for any subject area as in individualized instruction. However, the student selects that material from the subject matter which he desires to study, designs his own course of study and evaluates his own success or failure. The teacher serves the student as a consultant in subject areas, as a resource person, as a manager of all learning resources—material and human—and frequently operates within the realm of a Learning Center. The teacher also serves as a multi-talent developer, as opposed to an academic talent developer, and as an assistant in the student's self-evaluation.

The major difficulty in this approach, as in the seminar approach, is role clarification. The role shift, particularly for the teacher, is somewhat radical. The student is faced with the total responsibility for his education as opposed to the more traditional arrangement, where the adult professional assumes the major portion of that responsibility.

It is not suggested that school personnel select one of these methodologies to be employed in the entire school. That would represent the same fundamental error we now make when we assume that all students should be subjected to the same teacher-directed learning program. Schools should employ all these approaches as well as approaches that represent combinations of these. A single course could be conducted using any or all of these methodologies. A single student might use all these approaches in different courses.

Other changes will be necessary for the maximum functioning of the school. First, a curriculum structure as already mentioned, utilizing the suggested approaches, cannot operate within the lock-step time limits now employed. Flexible modular scheduling will be a necessity. Second, grading in the sense that students take certain courses because they have gone to school so many years must be eliminated. Grading in the sense that report cards mark progress by percentages or letter grades must be replaced by real evaluation.

The self-contained classroom—when that form of structure is not a must—must be replaced with a team teaching organization. Each subject area would have a pool of professional talent to plan activities cooperatively and work with students. Staff talents should be exploited to provide the best possible experiences for the students. The practice of keeping supervised study halls and book museums must be replaced with that of providing Learning Centers (with student access at all times) and areas which provide for quiet, individual study, peer group activities and socialization and relaxation.

The segment of the program designated as independent study would be a "free" investigation or experimentation time. During this time, the student would be permitted to investigate and explore the environment of the school and its Learning Center. He would choose the activities in which he would like to engage, and he would be free of pressures, other than his own, to produce. The major reason for this segment of the program is to recognize and maintain, if not actually foster, that natural inquiry innate in children. This is, of course, the primary vehicle by which they have amassed that great fund of knowledge they bring with them when entering school.

The teacher-directed skill development program, conducted according to readiness level rather than chronological age or grade placement, should consist of two parts. First, the basic skill development tasks would be handled. This should include listening-and-speaking skill development as well as reading and writing. Basic computational skills and basic data collecting skills should also be fostered. The second part, handled in the upper elementary grades, should consist of a number of general survey courses designed to familiarize the student with general subject areas. Included should be a survey of each of the following: social science, science, mathematics, humanities, language arts, physical education, leisure-time activities and vocational education.

It is my feeling that this program can meet the educational needs of today and is, at the same time, flexible enough to adjust to future demands. The key to the success of such a program is student involvement in their own education, to a degree that affords the student a hand in determining his destiny. This represents an admission that the school should be concerned with students as individuals and be dedicated to helping develop as many talents as possible in each child.

These changes, this curriculum structure and these methodologies are fundamental for a school's reorganization. The basic goal becomes one of providing students with the opportunity to develop responsibility, self-direction and learning skills. The opportunity to develop these talents increases from the first methodology to the fifth. In addition, independent study, and to a lesser degree individualized instruction, allow the students to develop a realistic self-image, decision making skills, and, of utmost importance, evaluative skills.

This whole concept changes the structure of the school from one of overwhelming pressure on the student to a structure which recognizes that students are the primary reason for the existence of schools, and should be treated as such.

PRIORITIES DICTATE BUDGETARY CONSIDERATIONS

This reorganization probably sounds ambitious and

costly. However, a feasible and worthy plan is a legitimate and highly desirable goal for a school. In terms of cost, we cannot offer quality education to our most valuable natural resources at bargain counter prices. However, the initial costs that would be encountered would be minimal. Each school could reorganize administratively according to this model this year. This would assume no additional professional staff members, no additional materials and no additional buildings.

However, for the maximum functioning of such a program, new priorities for future spending need to be established. The following investments would be recommended for the future, in this order:

1. Hire a full-time, in-service director and provide a full-scale, in-service program for all professionals. With the new methodologies, the present staff will need training in order to perform satisfactorily. New teachers will also need training. This training will of necessity be a continuing activity of the school. The in-service director may also serve as the coordinator of community and district resources.

2. Provide more services to the teachers, such as increased released time to work with students and develop curriculum materials. This may necessitate hiring additional people for each department (See Chapter 9).

3. Hire more nonteaching professionals to act as counselors to students. These people should not be administrators nor be involved in mechanical tasks such as scheduling.

4. Employ instructional aides and paraprofessionals. These persons might be parents who volunteer to work in the school. In this event, a person might need to be hired to coordinate the volunteer effort.

5. Provide additional materials and buildings as needs arise and after the other priorities have been met.

The program that has been outlined here is feasible for any high school or junior high school. It would, of course, be most meaningful if the elementary program could be reorganized along similar guidelines, many of which have already been presented.

TEACHING ROLES IN INDEPENDENT STUDY

Independent study, as an educational program, has become a nebulous, all-inclusive title for all activities which take place outside formal classroom instruction. In general, most independent study programs found in the public schools are designed to structure the students' unscheduled or study hall time. Statements such as, "Your independent study assignment for tomorrow is . . .," are quite common. Such an assignment is hardly "independent." Rather, these assignments usually take the form of homework, projects or contract agreements, depending upon the amount of time a student is expected to spend on them.

The role of the teacher in relation to these "independent study" assignments might be generally described as "director of learning activities." Assignments are given, they are checked and grades are assigned by the teacher. In this respect, the teacher's role differs little from that of the teacher before the concept of independent study was prevalent.

Perhaps a chart would help clarify this. Below are listed these three common activities referred to as independent study and the characteristics of each. Note particularly the role of the teacher or the teaching team.

UNSCHEDULED TIME USAGE

	Level I—Homework	Level II—Project
Student Role	Complete work by next class meeting.	Complete work by prearranged date.
Independent Choices Allowed to Student	Perhaps, but not usually, a choice of topic.	Choice of topic within subject area and where to study—lab, library, etc.

Teacher Role	Direct learning and enforce assignments.	Direct learning, suggest possible topics, arrange for freedom of movement by student and enforce assignments.
Evaluation	By teacher or team.	By teacher or team.

Student Role	Level III-Contract Complete work at own speed, within limits.
Independent Choices Allowed to Student	Choice of time, pacing and where to study.
Teacher Role	Direct learning, arrange for freedom of movement by student, serve as consultant to student and enforce the contract.
Evaluation	By teacher or team.

Variations at each level, of course, can be found in many schools. For example, students are often used in evaluating classwork.

It would be difficult to accept any of these three above-mentioned activities as examples of independent study in the strict sense of the word. Independence implies freedom— thinking or acting with a minimum of outside influence.

Homework, project work or contract work do not allow for, or even tolerate, freedom on the part of the student.

In most public school systems, the concept of student freedom is an extremely threatening idea—threatening to tradition, to the community, to the staff and to the students themselves. It is at this point, the dealing with threat, that team teaching becomes a significant factor in an independent program.

What might a true independent study program look like? First of all, all work done by students is self-assumed. If the practice of giving and enforcing assignments persists in an independent study program, independence on the part of the students, which is an acquired skill, cannot develop. Secondly, the evaluation of the self-assumed work must be done by the student himself. If the teaching team insists upon retaining the right to evaluate, students will continue to look to the teachers for direction. Thirdly, the student must be given the freedom to schedule his own activities and time. Without these options, the spirit of the program is violated.

The "threat" of an independent study program such as this is rather obvious. By asking a teacher or a teaching team not to give assignments, not to assign grades and/or not to require class attendance, the common and traditional definition of "teacher" is changed. In the public schools, nothing is so threatening to a staff as change, particularly a change in its professional role.

Role change by one teacher, a teaching team or an entire staff needs a supportive climate in order to progress. If teachers are to attempt any innovation, including independent study, they must feel comfortable in experimenting with the innovation and feel secure in knowing that if mistakes are made, that support will not be withdrawn.

A teacher working within a team is assured of support in attempting independent study if two conditions exist: first, if the program has been mutually planned by the team, and, secondly, if the principal is a working member of the team during the planning. In addition to the climate of support created by team teaching efforts in an independent study program, the individual teacher also benefits from the professional sharing of feelings and ideas with other team members, which is quite an innovation in itself.

There is no common definition of team teaching. Applications of the concept are as numerous as there are schools involved in such programs. It is difficult, therefore, to describe an ideal teaching team for an independent study program. If students are to be encouraged to do true independent study, as described earlier, in one subject area only, or at one grade level only, the size of the team and characteristics of the team members will vary greatly from those of a team which is encouraging independent study in all subject areas or on all grade levels.

Those independent study programs which cross subject lines and/or grade levels require interdisciplinary teaching teams. There tends to be more openness, freedom of discussion and willingness to examine professional roles and practices in interdisciplinary teams than in those teams made up of only, for example, the fifth-grade teachers or the geometry teachers.

A change of professional role would not be necessary in an independent study program, if the students involved were to follow the same lock-step pattern as is commonly required. Students who are expected to listen to a content presentation, complete assignments related to this presentation and take tests on this "basic" material in order to legitimize achievement need a system which is structure oriented and content oriented. Indeed, there are many students in the schools who will probably function best in this atmosphere (although this statement may well be a rationalization).

However, students in a true independent program do not need a content-oriented environment. In fact, it serves as a powerful sedative to the development of independence.

How might a teaching team go about organizing an independent study program for a group of students? Experience has shown that students cannot be told on Friday that they have the opportunity to be independent and they will become so on Monday. Rather, independence must be approached in a sequential manner. Three basic steps should be considered by the teaching team:

1. Orientation of the students.
2. Trial and error on the part of both students and team.
3. Productivity.

A more complete examination of each of these steps follows:

Orientation: The first effort by the team should be to explain to the students *why* the independent program exists. This involves a sharing of educational philosophy with students from which challenging and stimulating discussions and exchanges usually follow. It is necessary for the students to understand the rationale of the program if they are to be working partners with the teaching team in the endeavor.

Once the students and the team have an adequate working understanding of the purpose of the program, the team should introduce the options which will be available to the students in the program. Remember, if the students *must* do a project or *must* produce a paper or any of the other *musts* which might be contrived, an independent program does not exist. When *musts* do exist they should *only* act as guideposts of transition. Eventually these musts would also be dismissed.

Some of the possible choices or options which a team might consider for the students are:

1. Acceleration—content and grade level.
2. Changing of course sequence.
3. Changing staff resources.
4. Studying his own diagnostic data.
5. Moving outside the content area.
6. Guaranteed grades.
7. Self-scheduling.

Such a list of options could be limitless. The teaching team will be able to offer more options and combinations than can a single teacher, but this does not mean that one teacher cannot promote an effective independent study program alone.

The students should be allowed to offer options and should be encouraged to react to the list of options offered by the teaching team.

The final list of options available to students in the independent study program will be limited only by what the school system and the team feel can be tolerated. For example, a school district may not be willing to guarantee "A's" for independent work due to the external pressures of building class rank for college or selecting a valedictorian. In another case, the seventh-grade teachers are opposed to the idea. Regardless of the possible and inevitable problems which will occur, any teaching team can build an adequate list of options to begin the independent study program. The key to consider is *no* grades for independent study.

During the orientation phase of the independent program, the team will be called upon to establish a supportive climate for the students. This supportive climate will be of utmost importance during the trial-and-error stage to follow, but it must be firmly established during the orientation. The central idea is to make students feel at ease without constant direction and to be aware that they and the teaching team are partners in the program, equally sharing the successes and the failures. Establishing this supportive climate requires varying professional talents among the team members and the willingness of each member to be of professional assistance to the others.

Trial and Error: This phase of the program might better be called the "goof-off" phase as was briefly alluded to earlier in this chapter. It is the step which produces the highest degree of threat to the teaching team and to the school. However, it is an essential step in the development of independence and *cannot* be bypassed.

During the trial-and-error phase, the students will be experimenting with the options which have been offered and agreed upon by the team and the class. It. is highly unrealistic to expect that a student will examine the list of possible options, select the one he wants to explore and then move immediately to the productive state.

The early reaction of some or even many of the students will be to "goof off." Of course, when the students are accused of doing "nothing," the statement is made relative to what nonprogram students are doing—homework, projects or contract work. In these programs, achievement and progress can be measured quite easily. In an independent program, tangible "proof" of progress is not so readily determined. Other valuable learning experiences are taking place, however. Individual students will be examining personal goals and feelings. Also, it is at this stage that the students come to realize that the responsibility for learning belongs to them, and that if they do not "achieve" commensurate with their personal goals, it is their responsibility.

As this realization becomes an integral part of their value system, many will constantly pressure the teaching team for direction. In many overt and subtle ways they will ask, "What do you want us to do?" Of course, if the team succumbs to this pressure, a major purpose of the program has been defeated— the team is selecting the options for the student.

This is not to say that the team cannot offer possible alternatives or suggestions to the students. However, there is a fine line between suggestions and assignments, especially in the usual teacher-student relationship. Complicating the picture even more is the internal pressure the team will be feeling concerning the lack of productivity by the students. It would be so easy to simply tell the students what they ought to be doing.

Some students will move through the trial-and-error stage quickly—in perhaps four to six weeks, while others will work with this stage much longer. Most students will move back and forth between the trial-and-error stage and the productive stage many times during the school year.

A great deal of patience is required from the teaching team during the trial-and-error stage. Yet, the supportive climate has been established and the team can remain consistent with its philosophy; a new professional role has been learned and the independent study program is on firm ground.

Productivity: Once the orientation and trial-and-error stages have been experienced, students will move into productive activities, although all students involved will not make this move at the same time. For example, in a recent effort with independent study, one boy began productivity after four weeks. However, a girl in the same group struggled with trial-and-error stages for over eight months. It was extremely difficult for the teaching team to refrain from pressuring the girl by comparing her "achievement" to that of the boy. If this had been done, the girl would never have learned the self-discipline and independence which she now has.

The teaching team should be aware of and willing to accept the various types of productivity which will be evident. Traditionally, the only type of productivity accepted had to be tangible—a paper or a model. Other acceptable types of productivity might be:

1. Student attitudes have been improved.
2. Verbal discussion of activities have improved.
3. Self-direction or self-discipline is evident.
4. Student leadership has emerged.
5. Interest in a greater variety of topics is noticed.

These types of "products" cannot be readily measured by tests, so there is a strong tendency not to accept them as worthwhile of and by themselves without supportive, objective test data. Although most schools and teachers state that their goals include the teaching of self-discipline, improved attitudes, leadership and verbal skill, they try to teach these in a content-oriented curriculum which tends to relegate the goals to a secondary position in favor of content achievement. On the other hand, a process-oriented curriculum, even though it not only embodies the above-mentioned goals but places primary emphasis on them, usually creates extreme levels of internal pressure, and is, therefore, avoided.

Do not interpret this to mean that content is not important. Of course it is. But in an independent study program, process must be granted equal importance. Interesting to note is that in a recent experimental independent program, the students in the program, like the one mentioned earlier, did better on a pre- post- testing pattern (standardized testing) than did their control group, even though the experimental group was not required to attend class or take tests and was guaranteed grades over a two-year period.

It should be noted that the relative abilities of students have not been mentioned thus far. There is a general feeling that independent study is only for better students. Ability, however, is significant only in the productivity stage. The team will need to know a student's ability in order to make reasonable judgments about the quality of his products. But in the orientation and trial-and-error stages, relative abilities are not critical, and low- as well as high-ability students can profit from the independent program.

Professional roles at the productivity level are relatively simple. The team becomes a manager of learning resources, including materials, staff and community resources. It must see that all resources are readily available to the students. The team also serves the students as resource people, assisting *but not directing* the students in a variety of ways in their learning activities. The school thus becomes the all-embracing Learning Center.

In summary, a review of the professional roles of a teaching team working with the independent study program would be:

Orientation Phase:

1. Establish a supportive climate for the program.
2. Share the program philosophy with the students.
3. Explain the administrative limitations of the program to the students.
4. Build a list of options acceptable to the students, the teaching team and the administration.

Trial-and-Error Phase:

1. Continue to maintain the supportive climate, stressing that the "risk" will be shared by both the students and the team.

2. Be sensitive to emotions from the students, the staff and the community *and* learn how to handle these emotions.

3. Be aware that "goofing off" is a natural reaction and a necessary integral part of developing independence—be willing to accept it as such.

Productivity Phase:

1. Continue to maintain support.

2. Become a manager of learning resources.

3. Know the individual abilities of each student so that the quality of the products can be assessed.

4. Be prepared to accept different types of behavior as evidence of productivity, such as:

   a. attitudinal changes

   b. improved verbal discussion

   c. evidence of self-direction

   d. evidence of self-discipline

   e. emergence of leadership

   f. widening of interests

   g. greater self-awareness

   h. establishment of personal goals

   i. deepening commitment to beliefs and societal concerns

   j. other behaviors not measured by typical testing devices

In order for the teaching team to maintain the professional role necessary for the success of independent study programs, each teacher must make behavioral shifts. The behavioral shifts necessary can be roughly classified into five behavioral and attitudinal changes. The first would be a shift from the position of "the fountain of knowledge" to "the consultant" in subject areas. This involves listening to the student, accepting his interests and providing him with assistance in pursuing his interests.

Second, the teacher must shift from the role of "director of learning" to a "resource person." Most important, is the establishment of an "equality base" for student-teacher interaction. The professional will refrain from telling the student what to do but will assist the youngster in charting a course of action, once the student decides what he wishes to pursue.

Third, the teacher helps the Learning Center teacher organize learning resources. She abandons the job of being an administrator of a learning timetable. Further, she must be involved in an ongoing program to be "au courant" with the materials as well as district and community resources. It is her job to help make these resources gel meaningfully for each student in terms of his studies. Further, it is her new role to conceive of herself as a developer of many appreciated excellences rather than maintaining the single outlook of academic achievement as "the" worthy goal. These new role definitions for a teacher, of course, imply that how time is spent in school takes on a new face. A different set of priorities now dictate how time is spent. In addition, the teacher is no longer committed to the "coverage" approach to teaching and becomes rather a helpmate in the process of student self-evaluation. To do this, the teacher must develop skill in assisting the student to establish evaluative criteria for his activities. The teacher must learn to accept the criteria established by the student and judge the product according to those criteria.

In order to be successful, the teacher must develop skills such as, listening, dealing with emotions, giving support and developing individual rapport, to a much greater extent than these skills have been developed, or at least practiced, by most teachers.

There are many questions left to be answered concerning independent programs beyond the level of contract activities. Although there is existing evidence for formulating answers, it is not conclusive. The experiments with independent study have been too few in number and too limited in scope to make convincing conclusions. But as more schools become interested and more teams within these schools do experimental work, the concept of independent study will become an integral part of the school curriculum rather than an experiment.

Evaluating Learning Centers
and
Independent Study Programs

E valuation is perhaps the most difficult aspect of the Learning Center and independent study programs. "Gut-feeling-wise" so many
of these programs are so favorable that Learning
Centers and Instructional Resource or Materials
Centers are cropping up everywhere in increasing
numbers. Expanded libraries, additions to existing school facilities, remodeling and building
new schoolhouses with central Learning Centers,
all seem to be the latest developments across the
nation and internationally as well. Even home
Learning Centers are emerging. However, before
the accolades for innovative practice ring out,
more than positive "gut feeling" needs to occur.
Time and the results of current evaluative
research must be considered.

No ordinary evaluative tools are able to
match the task. Most school-type tests are
achievement or I.Q. oriented. However, since
none of the goals of a Learning Center program
indicate that quantities of information are to be
amassed, these traditional tests, therefore, are of
no significant help. They do not, for example,

163

test how much a youngster may have learned about Mickey Mantle or dinosaurs or the sinking of the *Titanic*. They don't necessarily test what a youngster may have learned about electromagnets or how to construct one because of a youngster's *interest* in electricity. Nor, do these tests necessarily indicate how well the youngster has proceeded because of his own initiative. To evaluate, therefore, special testing tools need to be constructed that determine behavior change. Also, tests may be constructed to indicate pre-project and post-project informational and/or concept development.

One evaluative tool would be the Attitude Survey as shown below. This survey could, of course, be altered by adding or subtracting items deemed appropriate by its administrator.

ATTITUDE SURVEY

NAME _____ AGE _____ DATE _____

SCHOOL _____ GRADE _____

	YES	NO
1. For most things, I do the best that I can.	1. _____	
2. For most things, I do better than my classmates.	2. _____	
3. I play games very well.	3. _____	
4. I play games better than most of my classmates.	4. _____	
5. Both of my parents have a job away from home.	5. _____	
6. Most people like me.	6. _____	
7. I have many friends.	7. _____	
8. I feel lonely much of the time.	8. _____	
9. I wish I had more friends than I do.	9. _____	
10. I am happy most of the time.	10. _____	
11. Others get better grades for work that is no better than mine.	11. _____	

12. Most of the time I am honest.   12. _____
13. Most of the time I am lazy.   13. _____
14. People can depend on me most of the
    time.   14. _____
15. Most of the time I like myself as I am.   15. _____
16. I feel that my parents understand me.   16. _____
17. I think I am important as a person.   17. _____
18. School is fun most of the time.   18. _____
19. I am going to quit school before gradua-
    tion from high school.   19. _____
20. I feel that I am doing very well in school
    this year.   20. _____
21. I could do better in school if I wanted to.   21. _____
22. My schoolwork is usually very interesting.   22. _____
23. My school is a good school.   23. _____
24. I like changing classes more than staying
    in the same room.   24. _____
25. It is harder to do my schoolwork when I
    have more than one teacher.   25. _____
26. Most of my friends like school.   26. _____
27. I would rather go to school than stay
    home.   27. _____
28. I like to go to school to be with other
    people.   28. _____
29. There are too many rules in school.   29. _____
30. The best thing about school is what we
    learn.   30. _____
31. I usually enjoy doing my schoolwork.   31. _____
32. I often feel tired at the end of the school
    day.   32. _____
33. I feel that I have to work harder than
    most students.   33. _____
34. I have more fun with my friends at school
    than I do when we are playing in the
    neighborhood.   34. _____
35. I have too much homework.   35. _____

36. I would rather do my own work than copy another person's work.   36. _____

37. I feel that I learn more in the classes I enjoy.   37. _____

38. I enjoy classes where I can move around in the room.   38. _____

39. I would like to know how to study better than I do now.   39. _____

40. I should choose what I need to learn.   40. _____

41. My parents and teachers should decide what I need to learn.   41. _____

42. My teacher should evaluate my program.   42. _____

43. I should be involved in evaluating my progress.   43. _____

44. I am responsible for my learning.   44. _____

45. Others are responsible for my learning.   45. _____

46. The teacher knows what is best for me.   46. _____

47. I would like to spend more of the school day in the Learning Center.   47. _____

48. I like being able to choose my own materials.   48. _____

49. I am able to work as slowly or as quickly as I wish with Learning Center materials.   49. _____

50. It is interesting to mark my work and keep a record of my own progress.   50. _____

51. Most of the Learning Center materials are interesting.   51. _____

52. Students have a lot of freedom in the Learning Center.   52. _____

53. I would like someone to grade my work in the Learning Center.   53. _____

54. I work best when working with others.   54. _____

55. I work best when I work by myself at my own speed.   55. _____

56. I enjoy working in the Learning Center because most of the time I can work by myself on anything I choose.   56. _____

57. I do better in the Learning Center than in the classroom.   57. _____

58. If you could choose your own project, what would you choose?   58. _____

   a. Getting information from library books.

   b. Doing experiments or going on a field trip.

   c. Art project.

   d. Performing in front of several people.

   e. Build your own project.

59. If you could choose your own project, which of the following would you choose?   59. _____

   a. Studying about something in which you are already interested.

   b. Studying about something you have never heard about.

   c. Studying something the teacher feels is good for you to know.

60. If a job needs to be done, you will: 60. _____

   a. Get it done quickly and well.

   b. Put off doing it until the last moment.

   c. Ignore or forget about it.

   d. Get it done quickly, but carelessly.

   e. Get someone else to do it for you.

61. Why are you filling out this paper?   61. _____

The above instrument is best used on a one-to-one basis between a youngster and his teacher. It may, however, be administered in other contexts, depending, of course, upon a particular circumstance.

Other systems of evaluating student performance, and hence Learning Centers and independent study effectiveness, would be based upon identifying behaviors indicated in terms of Learning Center goals and developing a method for determining desirable behavior change. Walter Johnson and Anne Kennard are presently developing such evaluative instruments, and it would be worthwhile to look for the research they had conducted. Their studies will be one of the more definitive ones in the field.

In any event, it could pretty well be predicted that present studies on evaluation would naturally hinge on a careful definition of terms or goal behaviors. Richard Bodine and Gary Lonnon, at the Lakeview High School in Decatur, Illinois, have developed a model for independent study and in describing it start out with their definitions as a natural prerequisite to studying their evaluative findings. They were indeed aware that independent study was a concept heretofore inadequately defined for purposes of evaluation. Further, independent study is a growing concept in education. Currently, this concept implies the occurrence of various student-initiated activities in a "free" milieu. In high schools, this "free" time generally means unscheduled time such as released time, library time, study hall, etc. Moreover, a careful analysis will reveal that high school students spend their unscheduled time in a variety of ways. For clarity, unscheduled time usage can be divided into three types. These types have the following characteristics:

Type I The work done at this level is teacher or team assigned and teacher or team evaluated. This encompasses most homework including drill, memorization, problem-solving, reading assignments, etc. These assignments have as a definite goal the minimum preparation, as judged by the teacher, necessary for normal student functioning in the regular classroom. The student has only the option, if any, of deciding where to study. The best label for these activities is "homework."

Type II The work done at this level is teacher or team assigned and teacher or team evaluated. This level includes homework that is deemed by the teacher to be necessary but which leaves the specific topic to the choice of the student. Assignments arise from regular classwork or homework assignments and are open ended, giving the student an opportunity to go as far as he desires, even though he is working within the framework of a regular course and possibly under the direct guidance of a teacher. This, too, is a form of assigned study. The student may exercise options as to where to study and, to a limited degree, what to study. This is "project study."

Type III The work done at this level is teacher or team assigned and teacher or team evaluated. A distinguishing feature is that the student initiates the assignment by asserting that he desires to make arrangements to study a particular area on his own. The teacher or team then decides what the student must do in order to satisfy minimum requirements for the content area being considered. Once these decisions are made, the student is free to go about his study in any way he chooses. The student may also be asked to evaluate himself. However, the teacher retains the final responsibility for the evaluation. The student exercises options in arranging his own schedule for this study, in choosing the sequence of the suggested topics and in selecting additional topics. This is "contract study." It may be used to take a course offered in the regular curriculum or a course not offered for lack of student interest. Programs which release students from class attendance but hold them responsible for what the class does fit this category.

It is difficult to distinguish between these three levels. Basically, the major distinction lies in the amount of time allowed the student to complete the work. Time allotment becomes progressively greater as one moves from Type I to Type III.

The Decatur Lakeview Plan, developed by the local staff in 1960, incorporates the assumption that a student should devote (on the average) 20 per cent of the school week to large-group instruction (lectures), 50 per cent of the school week to small-group instruction (discussions) and the remaining time to independent study.

The Plan involves team teaching and flexible scheduling. A large Instructional Materials Center housing faculty offices, audio-visual equipment with facilities that allow students to use the equipment and a library with individual student study carrels and student conference rooms are provided to allow for the independent study.

The Plan was fully implemented during the 1963-1964 school year. The large group, small group, team teaching, and flexible scheduling has proven quite successful. However, the independent study portion of the Plan has been most difficult to implement in accordance with the philosophy of the Decatur Lakeview Plan.

A survey in the spring of 1964 revealed that Lakeview students were using their unscheduled time working at one of the three levels previously mentioned. The feeling at Lakeview is that none of the activities at these three levels can justifiably be called independent study, even though students may be working in unsupervised areas. Independent study implies independent effort, but one cannot be independent in a meaningful way if he is doing work prescribed by someone other than himself.

Thus, a fourth type of unscheduled time usage needs to be defined. Type IV work, therefore, is characterized as work that is assumed by the student and work which is evaluated by the student. These two features are essential elements to any program called "independent study."

Incorporating these two features, a program was designed for students at Lakeview High School. This program was funded for two years as an experimental project by the Department for Program Development for Gifted Children, Office of the Superintendent of Public Instruction, State of Illinois.

For the experiment, two groups of ten ninth-grade students were chosen according to I.Q. and achievement scores. The groups were matched as closely as possible, one being designated as the control group and the other as the experimental group.

The control group continued in the normal program at Lakeview High School. The experimental group was placed in a program having the following characteristics:

A. Students were released from required attendance in mathematics, English, social studies and science. (Many were also able to arrange to take foreign language, business education, etc., independently, thus leaving only physical education as a course requiring attendance.)

B. Students could attend any class offered in the school. (This was to encourage them to make maximum use of staff resources.)

C. Students were required to take no tests. (Subject area tests are for teachers to evaluate students. Students may take the tests at any time.)

D. Students were guaranteed a grade of "A" or "B" in all courses taken under the program. Furthermore, they assigned themselves the grade.

E. An interdisciplinary teaching team was organized to work with the students in regular seminar sessions. The team included one teacher of each of the four subject areas, a guidance counselor, the director of the Instructional Materials Center and the project director. The seminars deal with the process and problems of independent study. The students are free to use any teacher on the staff as a resource person, even though that teacher might not be on the interdisciplinary team.

The experimental and control groups were tested before entering the program and again at the conclusion of their sophomore year. The data from the tests, along with other evidence gathered during the two-year experimental study, were such that the program was continued for the original experimental group and two new groups—one at the ninth-grade level and one at the seventh-grade level. It is anticipated that new groups will be started each year. The selection procedure for choosing the new groups will be as varied as possible, in an attempt to answer questions concerning what students can most profit from such a program and to determine if there are certain types of students who cannot benefit.

Results of SCAT Testing for Independent Study Program—Control vs. Experimental Groups 1965-1967

Experimental	1965			1967			Difference: 1965-1		
Student	Verbal	Quant.	Total	Verbal	Quant.	Total	Verbal	Quant.	T
A	97	68	91	92	43	80	- 5	- 25	
B	92	80	91	94	51	87	+ 2	- 29	
C	80	95	92	63	96	83	- 17	+ 1	
D	89	80	90	90	97	96	+ 1	+17	
E	89	95	96	88	91	93	- 1	- 4	
F	99	94	99	97	83	95	- 2	- 11	
G	75	92	87	58	91	75	- 17	- 1	
H	99	99	99	99	97	99	0	- 2	
I	95	91	96	90	96	96	- 5	+ 5	
J	86	98	96	73	65	75	- 13	- 33	
							- 57	- 82	
Control Student									
A	48	89	69	52	68	59	- 21	- 21	
B	87	98	96	80	72	79	- 7	- 26	
C	80	83	84	76	79	83	- 4	- 4	
D	92	91	95	92	92	96	0	+ 1	
E	99	86	97	80	83	83	- 19	- 3	
F	96	99	99	95	94	97	- 1	- 5	
G	94	72	91	95	54	87	+ 1	- 18	
H	98	94	98	99	96	99	+ 1	+ 2	+
I	84	83	87	72	35	59	- 12	- 48	
J	87	94	95	93	85	94	+ 6	- 9	
							- 56	-131	

This information at least shows that the students in the experimental study program are doing as well as the students in the regular program with respect to achievement as measured by a standardized test. The experimental group dropped an average of 5.8 percentile points while the control group dropped an average of 7.5 percentile points. Other measures of the thinking process, such as critical thinking, divergent thinking and evaluative thinking, may produce significant differences; investigation of these possibilities are now under way.

The experimental group took the College Board Preliminary Scholastic Aptitude Test during the second month of their junior year. The results show an average verbal score of 88.2 percentile with a range of 62 percentile to 99+ percentile, and an average mathematics score of 90.5 percentile with a range of 66 percentile to 99+ percentile. (No comparison between groups is possible, since all members of the control group have not yet taken the test.)

Results of the IPAT 16-Factor Personality Test by Cattell and Eber— The Results of the Pre- and Post-Testing on a Personality Test:

Low-Score Description	Control	Experimental	High-Score Description
reserved	+ .8	- 19.7	outgoing
concrete thinking	+11.4	- 2.5	abstract thinking
easily upset	- 9.2	+ 8.9	emotionally stable
humble	- 8.0	- .7	assertive
sober	+10.6	+10.9	happy-go-lucky
expedient	+ 9.0	- 4.3	rule-bound
shy, timid	+ 9.7	+12.9	uninhibited
self-reliant	+22.1	+10.5	dependent
trusting	+ 1.3	- 3.8	suspicious
conventional	+17.7	+ 4.1	imaginative
forthright	- .8	- 9.1	shrewd
confident	+ 9.9	- 9.1	apprehensive
conservative	- 9.7	+13.5	experimenting
group dependent	+ 3.2	+22.1	self-sufficient

Q3   casual   +13.4   + 8.9   controlled

Q4   relaxed   + 8.0   +17.0   tense

(All numerical values represent a gain (+) or loss (-) in percentile rank.)

Some interpretations may be obvious from the preceding chart. According to the research, as reported in the *Handbook for the 16-Personality Factor Questionnaire*, other interpretations may be made. Some of these are as follows:

1. According to Factor A, the experimental group is less willing to "go along" with expediency and tends to avoid compromise. Also the experimental group tends to be more dependable in precision work and in exactly meeting obligations.

2. Factor B is measured by a power test rather than a speed measure and, therefore, will not correlate fully with intelligence tests given under speeded conditions. The results indicate that the control group has only a moderate tendency to have somewhat more morale, persistence and strength of interest.

3. The results on Factor C indicate that the experimental group has a greater tendency to become leaders. Criminals also tend to score higher on Factor C. Also, the experimental group should be able to adjust better to difficulties thrown from the outside.

4. Factor G shows that the control group tends to view themselves as correct in, and a guardian of, manners and morals and as persevering, planful, able to concentrate, interested in analyzing people, cautious and preferring efficient people to other companions.

5. Factor H indicates that the experimental group tends to be slightly more suitable for occupations demanding ability to face wear and tear in dealing with people and grueling emotional situations.

6. Factor L shows that the control group would have a slight tendency to be more easygoing, more relaxed, and perhaps lack ambition and the desire to strive for goals.

7. Factor M indicates that the control group is more introverted, has a temperamental capacity to dis-

sociate through some relation to an indulgent, protective family environment, is less likely to feel accepted by a group and is more likely to have suggestions to a group rejected.

8. Factor N shows the experimental group to be more accepting of people and more tolerant of their own and others' failings.

9. Factor O shows the experimental group to have a greater tendency to be successful leaders in face-to-face situations; whereas, the control group tends to feels inadequate to meet the rough daily demands of life.

10. Factor Q1 indicates that the experimental group is more well informed, more inclined to experiment with problem situations and less inclined to moralize. They appear more interested in analytical thought, in breaking the crust of custom and tradition and in leading and persuading people. They are more inclined to become executives and directors, progressive politicians and scientific researchers.

11. Factor Q2 indicates a high tendency for the experimental group to become executives, scientists and criminals. They tend to be significantly more dissatisfied with group integration, making remarks which are more frequently solutions than questions and tend to be rejected.

12. Factor Q3 shows that the control group will exhibit slightly more self-control, persistence, foresight and consideration for others.

13. Factor Q4 shows the experimental group has a much greater potential for becoming leaders and assuming jobs such as engineers, executives, salesmen and farmers.

For other information, please refer to the *Handbook*. Some other evidence that appears to be significant is:

1. Nine of the students in the experimental group hold one or more offices in student government or school-associated clubs; whereas, only two students in the control group hold such offices. This at least

indicates that the experimental students are not socially isolated and that their peers recognize that they have leadership abilities.

2. Both students selected as American Field Service candidates are members of the experimental group and, further, the top five students selected by a panel of judges (people who were not acquainted with the students) were members of this group. The selections were based on verbal responses to controversial questions. Only five experimental students applied. Both candidates were selected as finalists. One spent the summer in Greece. The other spent the school year 1968-1969 in Germany.

3. There has been a significant change in teacher attitude toward this program. Considerable doubt concerning the program existed among staff members when it was initiated. This year the interdisciplinary teaching team for the ninth-grade students is composed of teachers who volunteered, with no released time, to work in the program. Ten teachers volunteered.

4. Parents have wholeheartedly supported the program and have become, in many cases, our best public-relations people. Many parents of the new selections were very favorable toward the program because they had heard other parents talk about it.

5. There has been considerable carry-over from this program into the regular program, in that teachers are giving more and more freedom to students in the use of their unscheduled time. This is particularly true in the "low achievers" classes. A new program incorporating much independent study has been launched for these students, involving an interdisciplinary teaching team and daily demand scheduling. Most teachers are presently involved in providing independent study opportunities for some of their students. Several teachers have expressed an interest in an individualized instruction program which will get under way early in the 1968-1969 school year.

6. The students have exhibited that they have assumed

responsibility. They plan and evaluate their educational experience in terms of what is important to them, particularly in terms of college entrance requirements. They are consciously aware of why they do what they do.

7. The students all express positive attitudes toward the program. They exhibit a very adult comprehension of who and what they are and they know what they want and how to go about getting it.

8. Teachers have learned a new role. This is the role of "manager of learning"—a much more professional role than the traditional "dispenser of learning." A summer institute was held to train more teachers in this new role.

9. The entire staff is supporting an "open-building plan" which provides *all* students with an opportunity to practice self-direction to a meaningful degree. Many of the feelings that all students can handle responsibility are based on observations of the original experimental group.

One of the most important discoveries made during the first two years of the program was the developmental sequence that the students follow in adjusting to the program. In the beginning, the faculty felt that the students in the experimental program would move from the regular program into a short period of orientation and then immediately into productivity. Experience, however, has shown that a period of time exists between orientation and production. This period is vital and should be expected.

The intervening period has been labeled "goof off." Students suddenly find that others are no longer responsible for their education but that the responsibility is theirs. At this point, the student must face some very important issues. He must answer questions such as: "Who am I?" "What do I want from my school experience?" "What will be important to me in the future?", etc.

When the student has asked these questions and formulated some answers for himself, he then must examine the options that are available. In the Lakeview program, the student must consider the following options:

1. *Acceleration*—Can I move more rapidly than the other students in the regular program?

2. *Changing Course Sequence*—Is it necessary to study the material in the same order that others are studying it?

3. *Studying Diagnostic Data*—Do the scores of achievement tests indicate any needs that I should strive to meet?

4. *Changing Staff Resources*—Are there other staff members with whom I would rather work? Who has the most to offer? Are there community resources I should tap?

5. *Self-Scheduling*—What classes should I attend and when should I spend time in the Instructional Materials Center?

6. *Moving Outside the Content Area*—Are there things to study that are important to me but which are not normally studied in school?

7. *Self-Evaluation*—How will I evaluate my work? What is important to me? Who should I ask to assist me in my evaluation? What are valid criteria for judging my work?

8. *Guaranteed Grades*—Am I comfortable with a guaranteed grade? What do I need to do to feel I deserve the grade? What is the importance of grades?

The "goof off" period must exist. If it does not exist, then the students have not been given a meaningful degree of independence. It is a valuable, if not the most valuable, experience in the education of the student. Teachers should not become overly concerned with the progress of the students, at least in terms of productivity, during this phase. This period, of course, will vary from individual to individual. The academic achievers, since they are excellent direction followers, may well face the most difficult adjustment problems; whereas, the discipline problem children, since they exhibit a type of independence, may have less difficulty. Furthermore, there exists no definite division between "goofing off" and productivity. After the initial experience in the "goof off" stage, students may revert back to it from time to time.

Academic ability is a poor predictor of success in such a program. Intellectual ability will only be predictive of productivity. Since the independent study should have little to do with increasing or decreasing the academic achievement of the students, as measured in standard achievement tests, one should not expect the same kind or degree of productivity from the "slow learner" as one would expect from the "gifted learner."

This type of program definitely demands a different role on the part of the teacher. She needs to develop or possess a number of skills for this role. The teacher must have patience, be a good listener, be an expert in the supportive role and be able to recognize and deal with emotions. She must know how to find resources—materials, staff and community—as well as have the skills to assist the student in integrating these resources into meaningful form. Furthermore, the teacher must trust students. She must recognize that they have the ability to handle this kind of experience. This type of program must provide the opportunity for the student to make mistakes.

It is not the intent in this chapter to imply that all of the answers have been found. Some of the criticisms of independent study programs have been answered in part and more answers are being sought.

For example, the following list represents some of the common criticisms of independent study programs and the answers or feelings thus far identified:

1. *Independent study programs are admissions that teachers do not know how to teach.* If an admission is made, it is that all we know how to teach is present knowledge and our real responsibility is to equip students to become professional learners so that they may deal with new knowledge. This demands a new approach to education—a new teacher-student relationship.

2. *Independent study programs are simply devices to relieve teacher obligations to students.* The demands the student makes on the teacher, particularly in the early stages, require much more of the teacher than in other programs. However, the demands are such that they require a different role on the part of the teacher.

3. *Independent study programs are essentially intradisciplinary and not interdisciplinary, thus discouraging application.* This is a danger if the program deals with only one content area.

4. *Independent study is intended only for a special segment of the population (gifted, highly talented, etc.)* Academic ability is not a good predictor of success and it may well be that the academically talented students will have more difficulty in adjusting. They are generally the "good" direction followers.

5. *Independent study programs tend to make students antisocial.* As mentioned previously, this has not been found to be the case.

6. *Students must possess all of the skills to be learned through a program before they are allowed to take part.* They do not need to possess these skills, as they can be learned. However, selection procedures have generally been employed to find students with such skills.

7. *Independent study programs do not teach the "basics."* The results on standardized achievement tests seem to refute this.

In summary, independent study will provide students with the opportunity to develop self-direction and independence, develop responsibility and learn how to learn. These things are not things that can be taught in the traditional sense of teaching, but rather things that can be learned in an atmosphere where mistakes are tolerated and even expected, and where professional assistance is available.

STUDENT, TEACHER AND PARENT EVALUATION OF LEARNING CENTER PROGRAMS FOR INDEPENDENT STUDY

While I was Learning Center director at Ridge School in Elk Grove, the need was felt to survey the students' and teachers' reactions to the Learning Center program developed in that 1967-1968 school year. The student evaluative tool was given to 422 first- through fifth-grade students. The stencil was cut on a primary typewriter with the spaces for YES and NO replies on either side of the question, thus facilitating easy replies from the youngsters. After each class completed the survey, the Learning Center aide tallied the results by first placing the YES columns side by side and counting across and then the NO columns. The following is the:

STUDENT EVALUATION

of the

RIDGE LEARNING CENTER 1967-1968

YES		NO
374	Do you like this year's Learning Center program?	42
325	Do you like having visitors in the Learning Center?	86
214	Have you gotten to use the Learning Center as much as you would like?	104
236	Do you like Interest Study better than working on subject areas for self-improvement?	124*
164	Do you like the idea of being sent from your math class to do math or from your reading class to do reading?	97*
292	Would you like to know what you will be studying before it comes up in your classes so you can learn about it in advance in the Learning Center?	55*

305 Do you find the Goal Cards helpful to you?   109

333 Have you gotten as much help as you would   87
like?

351 Does Miss Glasser seem to understand what is   62
important to you?

374 Do you think your teacher likes the Learning   42
Center?

373 Do you like making up your own mind about   47
what materials you will use?

253 Do you behave better in the Learning Center   98(*)
than in your classroom?

242 Do you think this year's Learning Center   67
program has helped you to improve more than
last year's program?

412 Have you answered these questions honestly   8
and carefully?

What ways could the Learning Center be
improved?

_____

_____

422 first-fifth graders responded.
*   59 first graders were not asked these questions.
(*) Upon request of the first-grade teachers, this
question read: Do you behave the same in the
Learning Center as you do in your classroom?

Another type of evaluation involving the students is
surveying their estimation of the materials available. Such an
instrument was designed by Jack Arbanas at the North School
in Glencoe, Illinois. See Figure 8-1.

As an addition to Mr. Arbanas' survey one could add:
Which materials have you given a fair try and think are poor? In
any event, it should serve as another idea in the process of
evaluating.

In terms of teachers evaluating the Learning Center

and/or independent study program, the following form may suggest some ideas:

TEACHER EVALUATION
of the
RIDGE LEARNING CENTER 1967-1968

YES   NO

11 Has the Library-Learning Center improved *con-*   1
— *siderably* during the course of this year?

 6 Do your youngsters like this year's Center   3
— program better than last?

15 Are you glad to have learned more about the   0
— materials; i.e., does this knowledge aid you as a
teacher?

15 Do you have a positive reaction to the Learn-   0
— ing Center teacher coming to your classroom
every other month to discuss the Goal Cards,
new materials and procedures?

12 Do you see the Goal Cards as a useful tool in   2
— guiding the youngsters' Learning Center program?

13 Have the Learning Center aides been helpful to   0
— you?

 7 Do you have a different idea as to what a   6
— Learning Center is than you did in September?

(Please do not mark YES or NO if you feel the
following question does not apply to you.)

 2 Have you taught library science more this year   4
— than any other year?

 8 Do you feel the staff as a whole should give a   4
— higher priority to the teaching of library
science?

11 Would you say there's a relaxed, but produc-   4
— tive, atmosphere in the Learning Center?

Suggestions: _____

_____

Positive Comments: _____

_____

Note: *15 teachers responded.*

Parent evaluations of a Learning Center program for independent study could follow similar formats. Another idea is as follows. It was developed for the PTA by Aurora's (Illinois) Learning Center Directors.

WHAT IS YOUR LCIQ?

(Learning Center Intelligence Quotient)

Circle the correct answer.

1. What is a Learning Center?

   a. An audio-visual resource center.
   b. A room for large-group instruction.
   c. An independent study center for individualized learning.
   d. A library.

2. What is the main purpose of a Learning Center?

   a. To give teachers more coffee breaks.
   b. To individualize instruction and develop self-directed learning.
   c. To give remedial help to students who need it.
   d. To spend more of the taxpayer's money.
   e. To provide a place where gifted students may go to expand their knowledge.

Name_____

Date_____

Program or equipment used	How often each wk.	Total amt. of time in minutes	Do you like it:				Would you like:		
			Very much	Quite well	A little	Not at all	More time	Less time	Neither
(Example) SRA Study Skills									
Special Projects:									
Comments or Suggestions:									

FIGURE 8-1

3. Who uses the Learning Center?

   a. Children who are through with their work and have nothing to do.
   b. Children who are working on special projects in their room.
   c. All children at different times throughout the school week.
   d. Gifted children who need enrichment.
   e. Children who need extra help in a particular subject area.

4. How does the classroom teacher use the Learning Center?

   a. As a means of individualizing instruction in the classroom.
   b. As a place to send students who misbehave in the classroom.
   c. As a means of supplementing classroom instruction.
   d. To take the place of classroom instruction in a particular subject.
   e. a and c above.
   f. a, c and d above.
   g. All of the above.

5. What kinds of materials are used in the center?

   a. The same materials that are used in the classroom but at each student's own level.
   b. Busy-work to keep the student occupied.
   c. Basic materials that are not the same as those used in the classroom.
   d. Materials that a student can work on at his own interest level and rate.

6. What is the Learning Center director's role in working with the student?

   a. To tell the student what he should do when he comes to the Center.
   b. To guide each student in an individual program best suited to his needs.

     c.   To evaluate the student's progress by giving him a grade for his work in the center.

     d.   To keep the students quiet when they are in the Center.

7. What is the Learning Center director's role in working with teachers?

     a.   To work cooperatively with each teacher in meeting the individual needs of each student.

     b.   To make teachers aware of materials being used in the center.

     c.   To discuss with teachers the individual progress of each student.

     d.   All of the above.

8. Which of these statements is true about Learning Centers?

     a.   Learning Centers are a new innovation that has not been tried before.

     b.   Learning Centers were developed when permissiveness was popular in school.

     c.   The concept of Learning Centers is relatively new, but has been used effectively in some schools.

     d.   Application of how children learn is not used in the Learning Center.

9. Which of these statements is true about District #59 Learning Centers?

     a.   There is one Learning Center in District 59.

     b.   Each school has one or more Learning Centers.

     c.   It is the only district in Illinois with Learning Centers.

10. How can parent aides and volunteers be utilized in the Center?

     a.   As clerical help in keeping records up to date, duplicating materials, etc.

     b.   As resource people to work with individuals or groups.

     c.   As library aides in processing and shelving books.

d.   As help in operating equipment and answering questions concerning material.
e.   All of the above.
f.   None of the above.

100-80   You must be a Learning Center director.
80-60   You've got the idea; keep going.
60-50   You need to learn more about the Center.
50- 0   You really should visit the Center more often.

Answers: *1.(c) 2.(b) 3.(c) 4.(e) 5.(d) 6.(b) 7.(d) 8.(c) 9.(b) 10.(e).*

THE RESULTS

Summarizing this chapter, the development of independent study programs at both elementary and high school levels, with "slow" as well as "gifted" students and all ranges of in-betweens, is a healthy, productive turn in educational history. Also, such programs naturally depend on facilities such as Learning Centers. Finally, from all sources such as parent (as indicated in a 1968-1969 survey in Elk Grove), teacher and student, all reactions are exceedingly positive toward this direction in education.

9

The Learning Center
of the Future

Boredom, underachievement (failure), hostility, negative work values are common circumstances prevalent among too many youths in our schools today. Educators could be accused of condescension in attempting to alter such circumstances. They may be told, in other words, "Don't bow to the idea of change... what was good enough for me is good enough for my kids." It would be more precise to say, however, that many educators cannot "stand pat" because quite simply they are attuned to the reality of present circumstances, and are consequently moving in several directions for healthy change. These broad areas of change are having effects that can be seen through: education's respect for innovation; the very slow but evolving teachers' role from being a purveyor of knowledge to that of a motivator, a guidance counselor and a member of a team; the design changes in our more "modern" schools; the extension of special services; the development of Learning Centers; etc. Guidelines with which to advance learning have, therefore, become: that which works; that which youngsters enjoy; that which can be promoted by honest reasoning; etc. These guidelines evolve into highly sound criteria the more we learn and hearken to what we know of human behavior and its development. Giving substance and support to this approach is the dynamic and vastly influential effect upon educators who are students of the noted psychologists and psychiatrists in this and other countries. Their studies regarding human behavior, its development, society's effects upon behavior, its growth through "self" and "other" acceptance and through group process—group therapy—are immensely exciting and cannot and have not been ignored by informed educators. Maslow, Piaget, Glasser (unrelated to the author), Rogers, Bettleheim and many other researchers are having a tremendous and indeed positive impact upon education today.

To overcome the unhappy circumstances our youths find themselves in while attending school, educators must dream dreams, invent and innovate. While it is true that little that is thoroughly new is being done, nonetheless, what is a frontier perhaps is how educators attempt to take the worthwhile things that have been done and adapt them, embellish them and organize them to meet the vast demands of a key goal in education—to tailor instruction to meet the needs of each and every child in our schools. Compound that worthy goal with the literal millions of young people to be educated in comparison to the piddling thousands of yesteryear, and you have merely begun to magnify the challenge of those who work toward this goal of individualization—and we can certainly have no less a goal.

INDEPENDENT STUDY—A MAJOR FACTOR IN THE SCHOOLS OF TOMORROW

A parent recently said, "Why all this fuss about independent study?. . .if I wanted my children to learn independently I could just as well keep them at home." Easily overlooked, as indicated by such a question, is that the elementary schools are of course doing considerably more than the important task of developing channels for learning through independent study. Professionals are available to provide special services; such as, psychological testing; guidance direction for emotionally disturbed and other handicapped youngsters; special personnel to teach the educably mentally handicapped (EMH); social workers; nurses; psychologists; learning disability remediationists; art and music personnel; the regular classroom teacher. In addition, the schools with Learning Centers provide a quantity and variety of materials and equipment way beyond the pocketbook of even a well-to-do family. Also, learnings in such areas as social studies, science and physical education still continue to provide the important opportunity for youngsters to learn through small- and large-group process, peer group interaction, sharing bits of information that each have gathered—all of which are guided by the teacher. Further, in schools exhibiting avant-garde leadership, studies concerning the worthiness of self and of others have become a daily and indeed intrinsic part of the school program, with this latter study pointing to the most important goal of all—helping youngsters toward the development of a positive self-concept. And where have we come to know the value of this goal better perhaps than in our cities' ghetto schools? From that experience, those concerned have had their eyes opened to the fact that when an individual has a meager, negative self-image, learning in school is a near impossibility. The next relationship came easily. We learned that not only were our ghetto youngsters thus suffering but oddly, and with little surprise, so too were youngsters everywhere, though perhaps not so obviously nor so severely.

Independent study therefore comes into the picture not really or simply, and by no means solely, as an expedient to coping with educating the vast multitudes, but rather as a goal in itself. As a goal, it seems to flow naturally from the one regarding the development of a positive self-concept. Fortunately, we see the tide turning toward these goals. The focus of education is indeed changing—growth prodded by a clearer understanding concerning human behavior—and, to such a degree that it can be said that this direction has been a gift to our time. It seems that more though not nearly enough people are coming to know the whys and wherefores of themselves more clearly. Nonetheless, we are not quite so isolated as was Emerson when he struggled for his selfhood which as he indicated, has as its reward self-reliance. (It may be interesting here to note that this journey to self, a solitary one, allows only that the experience remains sharable.)

The demands made upon Emerson and upon any individual who seeks a positive self-concept can be exemplified best perhaps by what Emerson, himself, said:

> What I must do is all that concerns me, not what the people think. This rule, equally arduous in actual and in intellectual life, may serve for the whole disfunction between greatness and meanness. It is the harder, because you will always find those who think they know what is your duty better than you know it. It is easy in the world to live after the world's opinion; it is easy in solitude to live after our own; but the great man is he who in the midst of the crowd keeps with perfect sweetness the independence of solitude.

While the idea being suggested here may to some express libertinism, such is actually not the case. Having a positive self-concept, being able to be independent and/or self-reliant does indeed imply the strictest code of responsible, yet, yes—free behavior. Quite similar is the democratic ideal of freedom—meaning freedom pursuable or existing as a result of responsible action, not at all meaning freedom to do anything you please. The key here, however, is an awareness that to pursue self-knowledge one must be quite able to study independently—alone—the only ultimate route.

And so we are led to perhaps the most important outcome of independent study—to bring earlier in life the discipline and knowledge required to make possible that solitary journey to self. It is without question the highest form of independent study.

In a sense, independent study can therefore be called a method to achieve the larger goal of attaining a self-concept. Independent study, then, becomes not just an expedient of mass education but more. . .an ethical, quite tenable means to an exciting outcome of the educative process—a goal which, when achieved, carries with it such rewards as an increased ability to use one's talents creatively, a sense of freedom with no fear of the responsibilities that life imposes (responsibility becomes much easier to assume) and the ability to truly love and find goodness in all humanity. Such outcomes are rich, real and presently more attainable for many people than ever in the history of man.

THE SCHOOL–COMMUNITY CENTER CONCEPT

Schools of the future are in the making today. Just as they are beginning to reach in and encourage man to strive for personal educational goals, they are at the same time beginning to reach out, which is a natural outcome of reaching for and attaining a self-concept—the ability to drop defenses and relate to others.

It has been common that schools have remained institutional islands, assuming such aloofness because they wanted to be the unchallenged decision makers of what the educational program was to be. They didn't want arguments. Issuing a new curriculum guide or a new textbook series was their narrow view of education but it is *not* what keeps schools vital and meaningful. Why didn't they want to open the doors to parents? Because they were simply threatened by possible challenge regarding what they were doing, and so were—or perhaps it should be said *so are*—teachers in such schools. Thank goodness, the trend is changing for whatever reasons.

A leader among districts for establishing a school-community plan is Flint, Michigan. With the support of the Mott Foundation, they built over a period of 30 years what has been called a lighted schoolhouse program. The local school building also becomes a community—a neighborhood facility making its usefulness an around-the-clock proposition. The activities that take place there in the evenings, and even during the day, are up to the families of the attendance area of that school. Sewing lessons, volleyball, baby care instruction, nutrition lessons, how to speak English, etc., are but some of the activities offerable.

Resulting from such involvement is a closer school-community relationship, bringing more harmony, more communication than such an organization as the PTA has been able to accomplish in inner-city and other areas.

Our staff at Grant Elementary had the opportunity in the spring of 1969 to determine what we thought would be a meaningful direction for our school to take. Several staff meetings later, it was determined that as a goal for our school we should advance the cause of school-community harmony—change the "standoffish" image of the institution known as school and seek broader communication in our community. (Again, PTA's as they now function simply do not assist very much in a communications capacity, particularly in an attendance area such as Grant School's, which as you may recall from an earlier chapter represents several cultural heritages and economic levels.)

Creating a friendly school image is quite important not only for the reasons indicated above but also, perhaps even more importantly, because of the effect it has upon youngsters. Parents who are more involved and friendlier toward school affect their youngsters similarly—an almost obvious conjecture, yet a proven result.

To begin to educate ourselves to this task, we called upon resource people for help, who graciously assisted us. Social workers from the Office of Economic Opportunity were glad to share with us their general knowledge concerning the low-income families in our area. Mrs. Leah Cummins, who is Elk Grove's Director of District 59's school-community program, also gave of her own time and knowledge. She brought to a staff meeting a film on the Flint, Michigan operation and advice to the effect that each school area must determine its own program—there can be no preconceived notions or ideas imposed upon the community. However, even before that could happen, communication lines have to be established between the school's staff and the members of the community. How? As a first step, through home visitation. The Grant staff now had to decide—were they really committed to the idea? The answer was overwhelmingly "yes," we *are* committed to the task of reaching out, saying "hello" and establishing communication lines based on honoring the feelings and thoughts of the total community—and all this with the blessings of our district's superintendent, Dr. Paul Lawrence.

Our next step was to seek faculty leadership to help organize for this undertaking. Mrs. Wanda Bather, an intermediate grade level teacher, and Mrs. Virginia Whitten, a primary level teacher, assumed this leadership. Furthermore, we have made ourselves aware that there could well be setbacks, but we have tried to prepare so that when they come, we will not be discouraged but simply realize that we must switch to a new tack. We are also aware that as primarily middle-class people, we need to educate ourselves to an understanding of how a different socioeconomic background will impose handicaps on our ability to communicate. If we reach out, nonetheless, with a kind hand and with actions that convey we truly care to be their friends, their youngsters' benefactors and that we appreciate and value their thoughts and their feelings, we just might succeed.

If we do succeed, what could happen?—greater use of the school facility, parent involvement during school hours, certainly an open-door policy, a parental-talent resource pool similar perhaps to the one developed in Winnetka, Illinois, parent-teacher committees for instructional advancement and something always dreamed of—pupil-parent and/or grandparent team learning.

Imagine for a moment! Is there such a school possible that could boast proudly of the following?

1. Relaxed parent-teacher-administrator-student interaction—a "you're welcome in my home," a "you're welcome at school," a "let's have a cup of coffee and work together" attitude—an atmosphere and spirit of friendly interaction for common goals.

2. Parents and teachers learning with their youngsters—many exciting things can be learned by adult and child together at school.

3. Parents and senior citizens using the school as a learning center for their own independent studies. (Public libraries would not be needed in practical communities if when building school-community schools, adult needs are taken into account. It would certainly be more economical to build a new school with a little more room and some duplication of materials from school to school than building a separate library facility. And irrespective of cost, this approach would be more desirable as a way of keeping the school's doors open to the community.)

4. Facilities for adult use such as a kitchen and meeting room, a sewing and knitting center, a shop, an art studio—all of which would be sharable with the youngsters.

5. Class meetings with parent involvement.

6. Evening class meetings for the parents and senior citizens, themselves.

7. Youngsters eager to come to school—no longer needing to say they don't like school.

8. Parents assisting voluntarily in a breakfast and/or fruit snack break and hot lunch programs.

9. Parents educated to not making an issue or conversation piece of the behavior of another's youngster.

10. A day care facility run by a community, not school, employee that is **not** intended as preschool.

11. Youngsters eager to learn as a result of examples set by both parents and teachers, and not from an artificial motivation such as being college bound.

The above-listed goals all have something very important in common. They result more from attitudinal rather than monetary circumstances. They reflect common concern, a deep caring about education—so much so that a united effort is forthcoming, an effort bringing much fun and quite satisfying fulfillment, as well as a highly mature populace, well on their way to making life a relished endeavor.

THE SENIOR CITIZEN AND THE SCHOOL-COMMUNITY CENTER

Senior citizen centers have cropped up across the country. These centers have tried to find meaningful uses for the time of our older folk. Very frequently, however, they have been understaffed and have not provided a meaningful outlet for a person's desire to live as productive and as meaningful a life as he can until he is simply no longer able to do so. A school-community center right in the mainstream of life would certainly provide this opportunity for usefulness and meaningful activity for senior citizens. The schools in Flint have started this trend. It would be well to see it actively flourish.

On July 10, 1969, the *Chicago Sun-Times* (3)* published an article entitled "Giving the Aged Purpose in Life" in their Cityscope Column. The article was primarily about the challenge of developing an active life for senior citizens. Robert Ahrens, Executive Director of the Chicago Commission for Senior Citizens and about whom the article was written, brought to light many interesting facts. "The science of aging is a brand new field," he said. "Even most colleges teach human development as if it ends with adolescence." Other interesting points were:

1. Emphasis should be placed on continuing education for senior citizens.
2. We ought to tap the reservoir of their talents, placing them in the position of being truly needed.
3. We should not "be overly solicitous and wrap them in plastic packages."
4. By 1985 there will be more than 25,000,000 persons in the 65-plus age bracket.
5. More and more people at age 75 will be functioning as if they were 45 or 50.
6. Foster grandparent programs have been successful and supported by federal funds to pay for their help.

---

*See Bibliography on page 221.

7. Persons 60 or older have been hired at $1.40 an hour to go to Cook County Hospital, Chicago State Hospital and other institutions to work with mentally, physically or socially handicapped children.

8. "People should begin developing interests in their thirties and forties that will carry them into retirement," he said. "I don't just mean hobbies; I'm talking about continuing education." Ahrens went on to say,". . .efforts should be made to abolish the idea that the early years of life are for schooling, the middle years for work and the latter years for leisure."

Mr. Ahrens' cogent thoughts are certainly helpful here as indicators of the naturalness, the commonsense aspect of school-community centers that are indeed for all—youngsters and oldsters alike. An even more exciting prospect could well be federal funding for employing these older folks as teacher and Learning Center aides. There is certainly enough research available to indicate that some very healthy, warm things happen when oldsters get involved with youngsters.

THE 12-MONTH SCHOOL YEAR PLAN

While this chapter is meant to be a dreamer's delight, nonetheless, as dreams go, the entire chapter is meant to be practical both in terms of educational goal fulfillment as well as monetary practicality. It must be allowed that in the process of achieving these dreams many tough hurdles would require overcoming. Perhaps it is necessary to accept the hurdles as an entertaining, though at times frustrating, condition for positive, desirable change, rather than being stumbling blocks for even contemplating a forward motion. It is too often the case that with an almost seemingly impossible, though indeed worthy goal, people will get bogged down and accept some lesser, more easily attainable platitude as a substitute for what they feel ought to be done.

A 12-month school plan is such a case in point. The hurdles are many and high. The possible outcomes, however, are many and worthy of the effort. As a school-community neighborhood center, it would seem that initially and operationally such a school would be more expensive than the cost of comparable facilities. However, it is also contended that it would be more economical, which is no small consideration. The following are the positive points for a 12-month or extended year's school operation:

1. Provides continuity in the educational program—no lapses or losses of learning over the summer months.

2. No work waste in terms of closing and opening school.

3. Better behavior continuity.

4. More students being able to use the facility would allow for a better equipped school.

5. Work would perhaps gain the perspective of being a pleasure-giving aspect of life, rather than one from which we need a long summer holiday.

6. And, as mentioned earlier, a more economic arrangement insofar as there would be: one building instead of two; two custodians (possibly even one) instead of four (or two); a school-community library center instead of a separate community library; community facilities instead of a separate community center, saving a neighborhood area of approximately 700 families about $1 million in taxes over a 20-year period after deducting the added costs of running a 12-month school; less expense in hiring substitutes.

The foregoing reasons are ample justification to work out the hurdles of scheduling, in terms of optimum facility usage and vacations for both staff and youngsters, to coincide with family plans. It becomes obvious that a computer service would be desirable.

The attendance area for a 12-month school-community center would be large enough to provide for 1,000 youngsters. A 12-month school would have two complete sets of teachers, a hot lunch program for both a.m. and p.m. sessions, ample opportunity for in-service education for teachers (plus college credit courses available as an extension of a nearby university's graduate studies program), computer service and three secretaries. All this may sound like a great deal—and it is—and still it is more economical. Furthermore, the multitude of added services to both the youngsters and their parents that such a school could provide would indeed make it worthy of a community's support. Add to those thoughts that a part of the teacher's daily responsibility is planning and study for the growth of the educational program, but not when she's dead tired after a long day with the kids. Schools under this setup could advance at a galloping rate.

Now to the particulars of the plan:

1. The attendance area could be divided in half, either right down the middle, geographically speaking, or perhaps preferably by having the proximate 500 be the a.m. session (the walkers) and the p.m. session 500 being the bussed-in group.

2. It would *not* be a "quarter-mester" plan! This 12-month plan would be based on a four-hour day (three for kindergartners) for 220 school days per year—which equals the present Illinois requirements of five hours/day for 176 days.

3. The children's school hours would be:

    Attendance Area A: 8:30—12:30—then lunch

    Attendance Area B:12:30—5:00—includes lunchtime

4. The regular classroom teacher's day would be:

    Attendance Area A: 8:15—3:45

    Attendance Area B: 9:45—5:15

    Gym Teacher A: 8:30—4:00

    Gym Teacher B: 9:30—5:00

5. A suggested list of vacations would be:

    February—one week (including either Lincoln's or Washington's birthday)

    Late March or April—two weeks (at Easter time)

    Late August—two weeks (including the Labor Day weekend)

Late December—two weeks (Christmas and New
Year)
Plus: two days for Thanksgiving
one day for Memorial Day
one day for the Fourth of July
one day optional
In whatever way the vacations were to be worked
out, the total time off should be eight weeks. A
district may wish to stagger some of the holidays
from building to building for maintenance reasons.

6. Suggested schedules are as follows:

PRIMARY

LEARNING CENTER—ARTS & CRAFTS FOR:

a. library book exchange   (about ten min.)
b. interest study   (about 20 min.)
   independent study
c. arts & crafts   (about 30 min.)

ARY A	MONDAY		TUESDAY		WEDNESDAY		THURSDAY		FRIDAY	
	LC Studio		LC Studio		LC Studio		LC Studio		LC Studio	
-10:10	2A		1A		3A		2A		3A	
—10:40	2B	2A	1B	1A	3B	3A	2B	2A	3B	3A
—11:10		2B		1B		3B		2B		3B
—11:40	2C		1C		3C		2C		3C	
—12:10		2C		1C		3C		2C		3C
ARY B	*Numbers=grades*			*Letters=each of three rooms*						
-2:15	2A		1A		3A		2A		3A	
-2:45	2B	2A	1B	1A	3B	3A	2B	2A	3B	3A
-3:15		2B		1B		3B		2B		3B
-3:45	2C		1C		3C		2C		3C	
-4:15		2C		1C		3C		2C		3C

Primary arts & crafts teachers 9:30—5:00 M W F; 9:00—4:30 T
TH; 9:15—10:00 adult arts & crafts, depending upon demand.

INTERMEDIATE

LEARNING CENTER—ARTS & CRAFTS FOR:

a.	library book exchange	(about ten min.)
b.	interest study	(about 20 min.)
	independent study	
c.	arts and crafts	(about 30 min.)

INTER. A

	MONDAY		TUESDAY		WEDNESDAY		THURSDAY		FR
	LC	Studio	LC	Studio	LC	Studio	LC	Studio	LC
9:15—9:45	4A		5B		6C		5A		
9:45—10:15	4B	4A	5C	5B	4A	6C	5B	5A	LC
10:15—10:45		4B		5C		4A		5B	
10:45—11:15	4C		6A		4B		5C		6B
11:15—11:45	5A	4C	6B	6A	4C	4B	6A	5C	6C
11:45—12:15		5A		6B		4C		6A	

INTER. B

1:45—2:15	4A		5B		6C		5A		
2:15—2:45	4B	4A	5C	5B	4A	6C	5B	5A	
2:45—3:15		4B		5C		4A		5B	
3:15—3:45	4C		6A		4B		5C		6B
3:45—4:15	5A	4C	6B	6A	4C	4B	6A	5C	6C
4:15—4:45		5A		6B		4C		6A	

Intermediate arts & crafts teachers 9:15—4:45 (adult arts & crafts teachers upon demand on Friday 9:15—10:15)

These Learning Center schedules are intended merely to indicate a possible method for providing all the youngsters with an opportunity for interest study pursued independently. The schedule is meant to be flexible with a free flow of traffic prevailing—if possible—between the Center, the studio and the classroom. Furthermore, this schedule is not meant to limit the Learning Center's use, though thought has been given to not overburdening Learning Center and studio personnel in terms of what may be called a back-to-back schedule.

The Learning Center would house the library, an A-V center, a librarian's station, a book exchange counter, some independent study materials, large worktables, chairs, a vertical file, a sink near the librarian's station, etc. The classrooms are to be considered subsidiary centers for quiet study. The classrooms will also house some materials and be accessible to other classes, perhaps by means of a rolling cart. When the classrooms are used, the teacher is an assisting agent to her students in their room. When the youngsters are using the Learning Center and the studio for interest study, the Learning Center teacher and the studio teacher assist youngsters at their stations.

The teachers will be the ones to decide where supplementary, independent study materials of a skill-subject orientation may be housed for greatest use and easiest accessibility. By teaming, by putting the materials in motion (on carts) or by opening the folding wall between classrooms, they can provide some solutions for optimum use of materials.

It is being recommended here, by the way, that there be two Centers and two studios in a building rather than one large one of each. It may cost more because of some duplication of materials, but need not cost more in terms of space—in other words, two medium-sized Centers instead of one vast one.

Each classroom should have a lounge corner like a living room. Carpeting throughout the academic building is recommended, and in the long run it has proven the most economical floor covering. Remember, the classrooms are an adjunct of the Center—in fact, the whole school is the Learning Center.

The librarian's job would not be to work with the youngsters. She would, however, train the teachers as media personnel knowledgeable in library science, materials operation and A-V equipment operation.

The librarian would supervise both Centers and assist the principal and teachers in materials purchase. She would have an aide working in each Center under her supervision. She would organize and supervise an adult reading room that would be near the intermediate level Learning Center.

The Learning Centers can of course be used by adults working with the youngsters and by youngsters for other purposes than interest study.

The Learning Center director's hours in an IPI school are

the same as a regular teacher. The Librarian's hours are from 9:00—4:30. The Learning Center aides' hours are 9:00—4:30.

PHYSICAL EDUCATION AND MUSIC SCHEDULE

ATTENDANCE AREA A (Walkers)

Gym A	Monday		Tuesday		Wednesday		Thursday		Frid.
	PE	M	PE	M	PE	M	PE	M	PE
8:40-9:10	4b	4g	1b	1g	4b	4g	1b	1g	4b
9:10-9:40	4g	4b	1g	1b	4g	4b	1g	1b	4g
9:40-10:10	5b	5g	2b	2g	5b	5g	2b	2g	5b
10:10-10:40	5g	5b	2g	2b	5g	5b	2g	2b	5g
10:40-11:10									
11:10-11:30	6b	6g	3b	3g	6b	6g	3b	3g	6b
11:30-12:00	6g	6b	3g	3b	6g	6b	3g	3b	6g

ATTENDANCE AREA B

Gym A	Monday		Tuesday		Wednesday		Thursday		Frid
	PE	M	PE	M	PE	M	PE	M	PE
2:45-3:15	4b	4g	1b	1g	4b	4g	1b	1g	4b
3:15-3:45	4g	4b	1g	1b	4g	4b	1g	1b	4g

Gym B									
2:45-3:15	5b	5g	2b	2g	5b	5g	2b	2g	5b
3:15-3:45	5g	5b	2g	2b	5g	5b	2g	2b	5g
3:45-4:15	6b	6g	3b	3g	6b	6g	3b	3g	6b
4:15-4:45	6g	6b	3g	3b	6g	6b	3g	3b	6g

g=girls   b=boys   PE=Physical Education   M=M

grades 1-6

The half hour scheduled for each class includes passing time.

LUNCH SCHEDULE

Gym A
12:30-1:00   Primary Attendance Area A
1:15-1:45   Primary Attendance Area B

Gym B
12:30-1:00   Intermediate Attendance Area A
1:15-1:45   Intermediate Attendance Area B

1. Gym B and gym teacher B are for adult service in the morning.

2. The classroom teachers would take turns supervising during one of the lunch periods.

3. Lockers near gyms for Attendance Area A youngsters.

Conclusion

This book has endeavored to make some specific recommendations regarding directions for education and, in addition, suggestions for implementing them. The methods, once again, are not meant to be inviolate but rather to be considered a starting point for teachers and administrators contemplating using some of these current educational practices.

As the basis for these directions, the following philosophical type of statement would be a guide:

AN EDUCATIONAL PHILOSOPHY

Our commitment is to educate all people—youngsters and adults—beyond such skills as reading, writing and arithmetic. It is further intended that our schools become Community Learning Centers where primary assistance is guidance oriented, with a minimal emphasis on the concept of instruction. Schools are to be exciting, challenging facilities for learning about self, all other facets of life and man's history. Further, schools are to gear their individual programs so as to enable men and women, boys and girls to become independent, mature, compassionate human beings, unafraid of meeting the challenges of life.

APPENDIX

From Library to Learning Center:
Tracing the Developments

The idea of having a library in an elementary school was implemented in the 1930's. A special room was set aside and shelving lined the walls. Books were placed in Dewey Decimal order. Usually, tables and chairs were placed in the center of the room so that a class could sit there during an assigned library time.

For years, and even today, the general concept of the library remains as a sort of house of books. Often quoted is the fact that the word library is taken from the Latin word "liber" meaning book. Therefore, libraries are frequently thought to be places solely containing books, pamphlets and periodicals—objects composed of printed pages and bound between covers.

The library concept, in recent years, has become broadened. Other avenues of communication are now associated with the library. A possible cause for the extension of this concept resulted from efforts to provide those who are sightless in our communities with some other means of enjoying a "good" book. As a result, story records, record players and earphones found their place in a library. From that point, it became logical to add musical records, poem records, tape recorders and tapes (when they

209

came about), collections of art reproductions, etc.

Teachers and administrators speculated upon these advances. They associated them with their pressing awareness of the multiple (and often complex) avenues youngsters follow as their individual learning needs dictate. Consequently, many schools were particularly sensitive to these advances. They saw that by increasing the media in their school libraries (few could afford to supply individual classrooms in such manner), they were increasing the opportunities of meeting some of the varied learning needs of their youngsters. (It may be noted that other factors influenced the development of the library concept. Technological advances, a need to make materials easily accessible and curricula changes left their mark.)

By studying education and library literature and various sets of library standards, the evolution of the library into a Learning Center becomes evident. New media now seen as key tools for learning and an expanding development of audio-visual centers in school districts and individual schools, brought focus on the library concept. The concept began to expand to include all types of materials and resources with many new functions and activities. This collecting and organizing of materials in a central location for more effective instruction has become the Instructional Materials Center or Learning Center. (The author can foresee a labeling of such centers in the future as Creative Study Centers.) To improve instruction, therefore, a vital need is seen to expand both in quantity and variety the materials available to youngsters. How these materials are to be used differentiates, in part, the Learning Center philosophy from that of school libraries.

The school library's philosophy as an Instructional Materials Center is set forth by the American Association of School Librarians and 20 varied professional organizations, which can be found in various American Library Association publications. The philosophy and objectives are widely accepted in both library and audio-visual literature. However, from the literature reviewed, the concept often assumed whatever title the persons involved chose to designate. The title **library** was fine for some, with a juxtaposed statement that it was now a place of extended services; others suggested the label **instructional materials center** or **learning center** because such terminology would indicate a coordination of many instructional services that previously were separate functions relegated to the library and to the A-V department. Regardless of the disparity between the name of such a place and its described and varied functions, the point being stressed here is that there remains little doubt that the school library concept is indeed changing from a house containing books to a materials center housing a variety of instructional materials.

There is but little question that the new library concept, the **Learning Center**, should be a thoughtfully organized area. Materials, instructional equipment, activity area provisions, quiet working space, should all be under the supervision of a person skilled in materials operation. Even more importantly, a Learning Center should be directed by a person—a teacher—with a genuine, warm sensitivity to youngsters who instinctively knows how to motivate them.

Some articles concerning materials centers seem to convey the idea that they provide a single service—one of supplying the teachers in a building with the materials and equipment they require to function effectively in their classrooms. Then, there are those articles which indicate that the incorporation of the A-V services with the library tends to expand and extend the qualitative and quantitative services of a school library facility.

Interesting to observe in these articles, is that the concepts indicated seem to follow two directions. Some writers believe that the function of a Learning Center is to provide youngsters with richer educational opportunities and easy accessibility to materials. The other trend follows the idea of a **learning laboratory**, where the key concepts deal with individual study and/or individualized instruction. The learning lab is organized by subjects and is frequently equipped and supplied to meet the district's curriculum design. It is set up for convenient exploration in such subject areas as history, science, art, music, etc. We see, therefore, that suggested are centers for learning and activity.

The new **library** concept—the **Learning Center**—appears to stress the idea of storage of materials for use by both teacher and pupil. Furthermore, it seems to act as a single unit rather than being an integral part of the total curriculum and educational program. Even though the labels, and perhaps the tasks, seem to be the same, there is one area that needs exploring. This area of exploration is the Trump Plan (named for its originator, J. Lloyd Trump) which strongly recommends a change in educational program and organizational pattern. The plan calls for the **Learning Resources Center** to be an integral part of the **total program,** not a single unit merely offering enrichment to the pupils.

The Trump Plan for Independent Study

> The heart of the school program is what is called independent study or learning. Here is where students, in addition to covering the subject as determined by their teachers, go beyond the minimum essentials to inquire and to create as their individual interests and talents dictate; they learn how to learn, and develop more responsibility for their own learning.

The foregoing quote is a goal statement. Trump says that ". . .today's teaching methods and school organization frequently get in the way of those pupils' goals. The typical classroom lacks adequate materials and the rigid schedule prevents effective independent study. This same schedule plus the usual teaching methods in self-contained classrooms, also keep most students from effective independent study in the traditionally organized library. It is difficult to get to the library; it is even more difficult to stay there very long."

The Trump Plan for independent study indicates increased opportunity for learning. It is meant to:

1. Provide for individual differences and abilities;
2. Meet the test of practicality; i.e.; the student is studying something important and useful to him;
3. Permit study in depth;
4. Develop the ability to go it alone, to learn by doing;
5. Produce in many students greater creativity and a sense of inquiry.

In line with an independent study phase of instruction, youngsters are to involve themselves in a project—one that they, themselves, have identified or one of a variety of project possibilities that their teachers have suggested. This particular project could be selected with a goal toward keener, more successful involvement in the classroom. The type of project and the sophistication of the student will vary with the time needed for a youngster to complete his project. Trump states that the extent of time a youngster is allowed depends upon the judgment of teachers and counselors, with consideration for parents' wishes. Younger students may, though not necessarily, be allotted less time. Trump's plan indicates that approximately 40 per cent of a youngster's schooltime should be used for independent study.[4]*

Trump's plan of independent study includes many types of activities; such as, reading,

---

* See Bibliography on page 221.

viewing, listening, writing, working on automated devices, etc. Many varied, supervised activities occur in this lab situation. Materials to implement these learning activities may be housed in one area (the Center) or in several locations throughout a school building and yet be considered a part of the Learning Center. These alternate areas are described by Trump:

1. The school library will contain reference books and other books of general interest, available on open stacks for use in the general reading room. Adjacent to the general reading room will be conference rooms for the use of small groups of students.

2. Materials of a general nature for viewing and listening will be readily available in special rooms, individual booths and in laboratories.

3. Individual student cubicles for use in private reading, writing and thinking will be near the library.

4. Student laboratories, with much of the equipment being portable, will be available for work in mathematics, the sciences, social studies, English language arts, languages other than English, the fine arts, practical arts and health-physical education-recreation.

The reading, listening and viewing rooms, the cubicles and the laboratories create the setting for independent study.

In his article "Independent Study Centers," Trump gives basically the same information about the areas but breaks them down differently. He writes:

Five kinds of facilities are needed for comprehensive independent study. How separate these facilities become depends on the size of the school, but one fact is certain—successful independent study requires more than the library, and more than an added room with audio-visual aids. The five facilities are: (a) the learning resources center, (b) the library, (c) the conference area, (d) the relaxation space, and (e) the formal study room.[5]

In this setting of various facilities—facilities which are spelled out in illustration and in writing, yet tend to be confusing—Trump states that independent study will benefit teachers and students in these ways:

1. Both teachers and students will adapt new approaches to student studying.
2. Teachers will suggest and guide rather than merely assign.
3. Teachers will become increasingly expert in getting students to use these facilities to the best degree.
4. Students will gradually increase their responsibility for reaching individual goals.
5. Students will learn to select and carry through projects and to show initiative in seeking study materials and aids.
6. Students will experience satisfaction in an environment that stimulates creative efforts.[6]

Trump calls the independent study phase of instruction "the heart of the school program." Although it is only one phase of instruction as suggested by Dr. Trump, independent study does include the four component parts of the school—the students, the teachers, the curriculum and the facilities.

Research on Independent Study

Little research is available as to the effects of a program of independent study at the elementary level. Literature on independent study is limited to descriptions of college and university programs and of a few at the high school and junior high school levels. At the elementary level, educators are energetically seeking to provide for individual differences and recommending various organizational patterns, such as nongrading, team teaching and individualizing skill or content areas.

Rogge[7] points out some of the questions pertaining to independent study. There are those

which deal with "who chooses what to be
learned; what activities do students actually carry
on; what expectations do faculty and students
have of themselves and of each other; what
products are produced; who does the evaluation;
what is evaluated; who participates; what resources are required; what is the relationship to
the total school program; and what research
supports the various models?". Rogge tells us that
at present most of the answers come from higher
education.

Bouthius[8] defines independent study as
both a philosophy and a method, which focuses
upon the individual instead of the group and
emphasizes the person-to-person relationship between teacher and student. Some of the first
independent study programs started as early as
1879 (University of Illinois). Many of these
programs started later in the 1920's.

A detailed description of the Trump Plan as
applied at Decatur Lakeview High School can be
seen in Chapter 7.

In his book on independent study,
Beggs[9] comments that ". . .the wholesale use of
independent study is a means through which
teachers can satisfy the individual learning needs
of students. It places emphasis on self-regulation
and self-responsibility for learning."

Jackson[10] reports on projects designed at
University of Illinois High School which seek to
improve instruction by increasing students' responsibility for their own learning. Students
studied problems of their own choosing and
sought to reach self-imposed goals. The students
believed such a project worked best without
supervision and wished for more places to work in
private.

Congreve[11] reports on the first two years
of the pilot study at the University of Chicago
Laboratory School, in which students in the pilot
group gained as much in subject matter mastery

as did the nonpilot group. Students in the independent study program formed a different relationship with teachers, regarding the teacher as a partner in the learning process and using him as a resource. About half of the high-ability students seemed comfortable with the freedom to work out their own program.

Several articles in the January, 1964 issue of *Educational Leadership* provide descriptions of the Learning Center, in which many materials are made available to students. Spitzer[12] points out the need for research, evaluating various materials as to their effectiveness and for what task. Krohn[13] describes the experiment in the elementary school in Shaker Heights, Ohio, studying the possibilities of pupils acquiring skills in self-direction and independence at an earlier age. Hock[14] proposes a broader concept of general education and a concept of specialized education as individualization of content and method. Emmerling[15] tells of a program to encourage independent study in the Learning Resources Center at Peabody Laboratory School of the Women's College of Georgia. Congreve[16] recommends the Learning Center as a catalyst for change in which "teachers develop opportunities which enable each student to proceed according to his needs, interests and abilities, allow the student to make choices about his learning and stimulate him to assume responsibility for his own development." Marland[17] in telling about Winnetka's learning laboratory at the junior high school level states, "The early adolescent child is struggling to separate from adult authority, to rise above conventions and to flex his individuality and autonomy."

Patrick[18] identifies three levels of independent study as: (1) seatwork or guided study; (2) teacher-directed assignments which are open ended as to how many ways you can solve a particular problem; (3) a program in which the student assumes responsibility for identifying his problem, topic or areas of study.

DeHaan and Doll[19] urge individualization of instruction to give personal relevance and thus release human potential. The relationship between pupil and teacher is most important.

Lindberg and Moffitt[20] say that if we "...truly individualize educational programs, children will be able to see their responsibilities in learning processes and thus can develop an independence that is dynamic and self-generating."

For decades educators have been talking about providing for individual differences, but little help has been given the teacher to enable her to accomplish this task. At present, new organizational patterns are being tried and new curricula are being prepared and tested, but we are still far from being able to meet the needs of the variety of unique individuals in our increasingly complex society.

A few studies relating to some of the differences which we may look for in researching independent learning may be found in research on exceptional children. One example is Siegenthaler's[21] study on the motivation of speech and hearing in handicapped children, where he found that the normal group of children chose as their first three areas of motivation: independence, intimate personal relations and group affiliation—in that order.

Burkhart's[22] study of spontaneous and deliberate ways of learning points out that the learning process is different for two types of personalities. The spontaneous learner needs information about standards, problem definition and self-evaluation activities. However, the ineffective spontaneous learner needs more purposeful work and help with sensitivity to expression and abstract ideas; whereas, the effective spontaneous learner needs nondirective guidance, sharing of success and failure and emphasis on the varieties of meanings. The effective deliberate learner is the pupil who needs to define problems rather than to give specific answers, who requires more personal expression and courage, who needs to develop new viewpoints by studying a variety of divergent topics and participating in evaluative activities. The ineffective deliberate learner also has a need for divergent topics and evaluative activities, but, more importantly, he requires personal motivation, courage and daring in experimenting, less initiative work and simple expressive objectives.

Bloon's[23] study on stability and change in human characteristics states that there is a critical point beyond which a particular characteristic is less subject to change. It may be that there is a point at which pupils must begin to assume responsibility for learning.

Gardner[24] reminds us that responsibility for "learning and growth rests finally with the individual. . . In the last analysis, the individual must foster his own development."

Perhaps a program of independent study will not only allow but also aid the child to attain this development.

* * * * * *

BIBLIOGRAPHY

1. Riese, Hertha. *Heal the Hurt Child*, The University of Chicago Press. (Chicago, 1966.)

2. Frederick Johnson, Architect 6124 N. Milwaukee Avenue, Chicago, Illinois 60646.

3. Reprinted with permission from the *Chicago Sun-Times.*_____, Cityscope Column, *Chicago Sun Times*, "Giving the Aged a Purpose in Life." (Chicago, July 10, 1969.)

4. Trump, J. Lloyd, *New Direction to Quality Education.* National Association of Secondary-School Principals (Washington, D.C., 1960), pp. 1-14.

5. Trump, J. Lloyd, "Independent Study Centers—Their Relation to the Central Library," *The Bulletin of the National Association of Secondary-School Principals*, 50 (January, 1966), pp. 45-51.

6. *Ibid.*

7. Rogge, W. M. "Independent Study Is Self-Directed Learning." In Begges, D.W. and E. G. Buffie (Eds.) *Independent Study.* Bloomington, Indiana: Indiana University Press, 1965.

8. Bouthius, E.H., F. J. Davis and J. S. Drushall. *The Independent Study Program in the United States.* New York: Columbia University Press, 1957.

9. Beggs, David W., III, and E.G. Buffie, *Independent Study*. Bloomington, Indiana: Indiana University Press, 1965.

10. Jackson, D.M., et al, "Five Projects Designed to Increase Students' Independence in Learning. University of Illinois High School." *National Association of Secondary-School Principals Bulletin*, 44, January, 1960. pp. 290-304.

11. Congreve, W. J. "Learning Center. . . .Catalyst for Change?" *Educational Leadership*. Vol. 21, No. 4, January, 1964.

12. Spitzer, Lillian. "Looking at Centers for Learning Through Research-Colored Glasses." *Educational Leadership*. Vol. 21, No. 4, January, 1964.

13. Krohn, Mildred L. "Learning and the Learning Center." *Educational Leadership*. Vol. 21, No. 4, January, 1964.

14. Hock, Louise E. "A New Conception of General Education." *Educational Leadership*. Vol. 21, No. 4, January, 1964.

15. Emmerling, F.C. "Salt for Education." *Educational Leadership*. Vol. 21, No. 4, January, 1964.

16. Congreve, loc cit, p. 212.

17. Marland, S.P., Jr. "Winnetka's Learning Laboratory." *Educational Leadership*, 20: 459, April, 1963.

18. Patrick, Anne. "Practices and Programs for Elementary Schools." In Beggs. D.W. and E.G. Buffie (Eds.) *Independent Study*. Bloomington: Indiana University Press, 1965.

19. DeHaan, R. V. and R. C. Doll. "Individualization and Human Potential." In Doll,

R.C. (Ed.) *Individualizing Instruction.* Washington, D. C.: Association for Supervision and Curriculum Development, 1964.

20. Lindberg, Lucille and Mary W. Moffitt. "What Is Individualizing Education?" In Association for Childhood Education International. *Individualizing Education.* Washington, D.C.: ACEI, 1964.

21. Siegenthaler, B.M. *Motivation of Speech and Hearing in Handicapped Children.* University Park, Pennsylvania: The Pennsylvania State University Speech and Hearing Clinic, 1960.

22. Burkhart, R.D. *Spontaneous and Deliberate Ways of Learning.* Scranton, Pennsylvania: International Textbook Co., 1962.

23. Bloon, B. S. *Stability and Change in Human Characteristics.* New York: John Wiley & Sons, Inc., 1964.

24. Gardner, J.W. *Excellence.* New York: Harper & Row, 1961.

INDEX

A

Ability grouping, 55
Acoustics, 55
Additions, 110-111
Aide:
 average staffing, 103, 104-105
 differentiated staffing, 107
 ideal staffing, 106
 minimal staffing, 95-97
 qualifications, 95-97
 responsibilities listed, 104-105
 role, 103, 104-105
Alcove, 120
Answer sheets, 67
Arbanas, Jack, 182
Art objects, 120
Artists, 28
Arts-and-crafts media, 28, 54
Arts-and-crafts teacher, 106
Attitude survey, 164-167
Audio-visual aids, 20
Audio-visual equipment, 118
Author cards, 61
Authoritarian teacher, 52
Autocratic teacher, 52
· A-V storage room and production
 area, 119

B

Basis:
 Elk Grove School District, 15-26,
  59
 Goal card, 23-26
 philosophy fulfillment, 26
 purposes, goals, objectives,
  18-23
 North School, Glencoe, Illinois,
  26-32
 behavioral objectives, 27-28
 comments, 28-32
 goals, 27
Beggs, 216
Behavior, controlling own, 27
Behavior-problem youngsters, 51
Behavioral goals, 27-28
Biographies, 61
Biography book card, 65
Bloon, 219
Bodine, Richard J., 135
Book exchange, 52
Book exchange counter, 120
Book slide, 120
Books, use, 52-53
Bouthius, 216
Brentwood School, 74, 81

227